# KEYSTONE BOOKS

# GUY DOMVILLE

*HENRY JAMES*

# GUY DOMVILLE

### PLAY IN THREE ACTS

with comments by Bernard Shaw, H. G. Wells
and Arnold Bennett

preceded by

## HENRY JAMES: THE DRAMATIC YEARS

### BIOGRAPHICAL CHAPTERS

by

*LEON EDEL*

## J. B. LIPPINCOTT COMPANY
### PHILADELPHIA & NEW YORK

Copyright 1949, © 1960 by Leon Edel

*Guy Domville* copyright 1949 by the President
and Fellows of Harvard College

First Edition

Printed in the United States of America

Library of Congress Catalog Card Number 60-13584

# FOR WILLIAM JAMES

this record of his uncle's

play-writing years

# CONTENTS

# CONTENTS

# FOREWORD

IN THIS BOOK is published—for the first time in a popular edition—Henry James's play *Guy Domville,* which all but created a riot when it was produced in London in 1895. The full story of this unusual first night was told by me in *The Complete Plays of Henry James,* published in 1949, when *Guy Domville* was first publicly printed—more than half a century after it was written—along with James's other unpublished dramatic works.

It is because this play had such a curious fate, and occupies so significant a place in the life of the novelist (as well as in the annals of the London theatre), that it is offered here in its full historical setting. I have revised for this purpose the biographical chapters dealing with James's "dramatic years," and have incorporated into these, in the section entitled "The Last of the Domvilles," my reconstruction of the events of the night of January 5, 1895. In undertaking such a reconstruction I was prompted—to a degree like Thornton Wilder's Brother Juniper—to discover the strange chain of circumstances which can lead to an ultimate disaster. My object was to explain the effect of the "disaster" upon the novelist's later works.

In order to place *Guy Domville* in its proper setting, it has seemed to me useful to add the critical notices written immediately after the first night by three comparatively unknown writers of the time: Bernard Shaw, H. G. Wells and Arnold Bennett.

I should add that the biographical chapters included in this book were written before my study of James's early life, *Henry James: The Untried Years,* and are wholly independent of the further work on the novelist I now have in preparation.

LEON EDEL

*Cambridge, Mass., 1960*

# I

# Henry James:
# The Dramatic Years

❖

BY LEON EDEL

# HENRY JAMES:

# THE DRAMATIC YEARS

## I. A SMALL BOY AT THE PLAY

IN THE HOURS before dawn of January 4, 1910, Henry James—he was then sixty-seven—sat at his work table in Lamb House, Rye, Sussex, scrawling notes for a new novel in a rapid, half-illegible hand across large loose sheets. As the balanced sentences formed themselves, exploring the plot, casting about for structural elements, gathering up memories, a sense of exhilaration swept over the novelist—the joy of remembering, assembling, creating. The manuscript pages, with their pencilled scribble, tell the story: the sense of creative strength, the gratitude, mystical and semi-religious, for the guidance of his "blest Genius," the surge of inner passion, the expression of tender feeling for a Muse—the hidden "powers and forces and divinities" at the sources of his art. The passage has all the quality of a prayer:

> I come back yet again and again, to my only seeing it
> in the dramatic way—as I can only see everything and
> anything now. . . . Momentary sidewinds—things of
> no real authority—break in every now and then to put
> their inferior little questions to me; but I come back,
> I come back, as I say, I all throbbingly and yearningly

and passionately, oh *mon bon,* come back to this way
that is clearly the only one in which I can do anything
now, and that will open out to me more and more, and
that has overwhelming reasons pleading all beautifully
in its breast.

Why was the "dramatic way" the only way? That is
our point of departure.

### 1.

Henry James was taken to the theatre at an early
age, and thereafter, for sixty years, he was a consistent (and consistently critical) playgoer. He was
a stage-struck boy, a stage-enamored young student,
a serious-minded drama critic, and in middle life
an anxious playwright. The theatre never lost its
fairy-tale spell for him. He might grumble at the
poorness of the play, sitting deep in his stall, his
eyes taking in every detail on the stage; he was seldom satisfied with the actors, save those of the
Théâtre Français; he tended to speak of "theatre"
as an institution created to "murder" dramatic
literature; yet, at the hushed moment before the
curtain's rise, when the new play opened, he was
there in box or stall, ready to renew the experience,
ready to sit glowing with momentary satisfaction or
moaning and muttering to himself, or, so it has
been reported, rising half-way through a play with
an audible "I can't bear it any longer," and stalking
from the theatre.

There were times when his attitude was less
overtly belligerent. Going to the theatre in the
company of actresses—the great Fanny Kemble,
Mary Anderson, Elizabeth Robins—provided ears
for his running commentary and opportunities for
the exercise of wit. Miss Robins has testified that
it required courage to accompany the novelist to
the play: "One never grew wholly acclimatized to
the nipping airs that now and then would blow

about the startled stalls. Mr. James's all too audible remarks, conveyed in terms always 'chosen,' often singularly picturesque, sometimes diabolic, as though he revelled in mercilessness—would send cold shivers down his companion's spine." Mary Anderson's testimony sheds further light: "He sat by me and whispered his criticisms. 'You see that fat, rubicund old Colonel on the stage now; well, shortly he is bound to say "Damn it, sir," and the audience will be delighted. Oh, they love trifles and vulgar trifles very often.' He had hardly finished speaking when the fat old Colonel said, 'Damn it, sir,' and the audience laughed long and loud."

If the middle-aged playgoer thus brought a personal bias and an intricate and highly individual critical apparatus into the theatre, it was because in mid-nineteenth century a small New York boy had been taken to the theatre by his parents with uncommon regularity, and because nights in the theatres of Broadway, Chambers Street and Park Place provided that familiarity with the "scenic art" which is a pre-requisite to critical theatregoing. Memories of childhood adventures in art crowd the 436 pages of Henry James's autobiographical *A Small Boy and Others,* a volume which covers only the first fourteen years of his life. Fully one-eighth of the book is filled with the names of plays and actors, what they wore, how they strutted, their very grimaces, as well as of the lamplit and gaslit old theatres—all recounted and pictured with an evident delight at seventy, although six decades separated the old James from the little New York playgoer.

He remembered how he used to wander down lower Fifth Avenue spelling out the names of plays and players on yellow and white billboards, pasted in those days on large screens leaning against trees and fences; and he remembered how he used to trudge up Broadway, his hoarded pennies in his pocket—walking to save the fare, averting his eyes as he passed the doughnut stands—in order to attend matinees at Barnum's "Lecture Room," to which little boys were drawn by the same magic that keeps little boys of our era glued to the television "western." Here the dramatic art was embodied for him in the person of such actresses as the red-faced Emily Mestayer, with damp ringlets and a "vast protuberance of bosom" playing in J. Sheridan Knowles's *Love or The Countess and the Serf,* shouting at the top of her lungs that a purse of gold "would be the fair guerdon of the minion" who should start on the spot to do her bidding. He remembered her also as Eliza in *Uncle Tom's Cabin,* "her swelling bust encased in a neat cotton gown" and her flight across the ice blocks "intrepidly and gracefully performed."

The book, the literary periodical, the concert stage and the art gallery, all held places of importance in the lives of the four James boys and their sister; but books could be read quietly at home, and pictures studied in picture-books or in a casual stroll through a gallery, whereas going to the theatre involved a trip in a carriage, an encounter, over flickering footlights, with strange and fantastic characters, and after the performance, recapitulation and critical discussion. Henry's parents, he tells us, had a simple theory. They liked the theatre— such as it was—in those early American days of lurid melodrama and elaborate farces, Shakespearian productions that would seem heavy-handed to us, and burlesque Dickens characters. They reasoned that if the plays were good enough for them they were good enough for the children.

But first, before Henry had reached an age considered ripe for theatregoing, there were allied pleasures: the pantomime, the concert hall, and, inevitably, the circus. Theatres came later. He remembered hearing the infant Adelina Patti, poised in an armchair at the edge of the footlights, warbling precocious notes; visits to Niblo's Gardens to see the Ravels in their pantomime of *Jocko or The Brazilian Ape* and *Zaoul or The Magic Star* (it emerges in James's recollections as *Raoul or The Night Owl*) and to Franconi's "monumental" Hippodrome, which rang with Roman chariot races. There was a visit to the New York version of the Crystal Palace, sprawled over half a dozen acres in the far reaches of "uptown" Forty-second Street, where it seemed to Henry James years later he got the first taste of a voyage to Europe, in the light of the Palace's Old World origins, so that the return in the autumn dusk on the new Sixth Avenue cars was a "relapse into soothing flatness, a return to the Fourteenth Street horizon from a far journey."

2.

He never forgot that his older brother Willam was taken to the theatre first. He has left us a record in two places of the incident. In *A Small Boy* the novelist remembers "having, in the first place, but languished at home when my betters admired Miss Cushman." "My betters" included William, who was a year older than himself. Ten years before this allusion, he had set down a fuller account in a biography of the American sculptor, Willam Wetmore Story, where a reference to Charlotte Cushman set him off on a digression that concerned his own boyhood rather than the life of Story. He and his brother, one winter's evening in their Fourteenth Street home, were doing their lessons for the next day; the parents were at the theatre seeing Miss Cushman in Shakespeare's *Henry VIII.* Suddenly the elder Henry reappeared; he had driven home from the theatre in haste at the end of the act, impressed with the play's interest for the older of the small boys. William was snatched up from his homework and taken off to see Shakespeare. The Henry James of 1903, looking back at the small Henry of 1850, is filled with pity and resentment.

> . . . The scene, that evening, at which, through my being inadequately estimated, I did not assist, is one of the most ineffaceable in my tolerably rich experience of the theatre. I recall it as a vivid vigil in which the poor lonely lamplight became that of the glittering stage in which I saw wondrous figures and listened to thrilling tones, in which I knew "Shakespeare acted" as I was never to know him again, in which, above all, I nursed my view of paternal discrimination.

Miss Cushman played in *Henry VIII* in September 1849, again in January 1850 and in June 1851 (always at the Broadway Theatre and not at the Park, as Henry recalled) and at Brougham's Lyceum in 1852. By 1852, however, Henry had been taken to the play and consequently the 1850 date—a winter's night—would seem the most plausible. He was then seven—old enough to sense keenly the "paternal discrimination" in favor of an older brother who would then have been eight.

He has set down in great detail his recollection of the first night of his own theatregoing. He believed the play was *A Comedy of Errors,* produced by William Burton in his small theatre in Chambers Street. The Shakespearian production Henry James describes in his memoirs, however, could not have been his first experience as a playgoer. Burton produced *A Comedy of Errors* during 1853 and again in 1855, and by that time the small boy had already seen many plays. The production he describes fits completely Burton's of April 18, 1855, when Henry was twelve. The novelist recalled that "a celebrated actor, whose name I inconsistently forget, had arrived to match Mr. Burton as the other of the Dromios." Burton was twinned on this occasion by the Dromio of Harry Hall, "an actor of good repute" newly-arrived from London. The novelist remembers also Mrs. Holman as playing Adriana in this production; she was, indeed, in the cast, but in the role of Luciana. The only other productions of the play during this time were at Barnum's "Lecture Hall" in January 1851 and at the Bowery Theatre in March of that year. 1851 could have been that of Henry James's coming-of-age as a theatregoer. He was eight and we have seen that this was the age at which Willam was judged by his father to be old enough to see Shakespeare.

He remembered that the play had been read to him during the day of his theatregoing debut; he recalled the "sacred thrill" once inside the theatre in Chambers Street before a green curtain that refused to go up: "One's eyes bored into it in vain, and yet one knew it *would* rise at the named hour, the only question being if one could exist till then."

We can picture the James family arriving at the theatres of old New York with their two older sons, during the early 1850's: the bearded elder Henry, descending from the inevitable carriage—he had lost a leg in an early accident and ever afterwards relied upon this means of transport—accompanied by his wife and two bright-eyed boys, attired in jackets such as Henry wears in a daguerreotype of the period, brass-buttoned right up to the neck, with only an edge of white shirt showing. Young Henry was taken to all the leading New York theatres of the mid-century—Burton's, the Broadway and the National, Wallack's Lyceum, Niblo's Gardens and Barnum's "Lecture Room" attached to the Great American Museum. It was the era when many theatres, in the lingering Puritanism, still masqueraded as gardens, lecture rooms, lyceums —anything in name but what they really were.

At Burton's he saw such familiar farces as *The Toodles* and *The Serious Family;* at the Broadway the super-spectacle of *The Cataract of the Ganges or The Rajah's Daughter* and the popular *Green Bushes;* at Wallack's the popular comedies of Dion Boucicault (James rightly recalls that it was then written Bourcicault), *London Assurance* and *Love in a Maze*. And always there is the vivid recollection of the actors: William Burton, the Aminadab Sleek, Mr. Toodles or Paul Pry, "his huge person, his huge fat face and his vast slightly pendulous cheek, surmounted by a sort of elephantine wink, to which I impute a remarkable baseness"; Madame Ponisi, the Oberon of *A Midsummer Night's Dream,* "as representing all characters alike with a broad brown face framed in bands or crowns or other heavy headgear out of which cropped a row of very small tight black curls"; Madame Céline Celeste, "straight out of London" in *Green Bushes* (J. B. Buckston's play which James wrongly attributes to Boucicault), "whose admired walk up the stage as Miami the huntress, a wonderful majestic and yet voluptuous stride enhanced by a short kilt, black velvet leggings and a gun haughtily borne on the shoulder is vividly before me. . . ." Miss Julia Bennett "fresh from triumphs at the Haymarket . . . in a very becoming white bonnet, either as a brilliant adventuress or as the innocent victim of licentious design, I forget which, though with a sense somehow that the white bonnet, when of true elegance, was the note of that period of the adventuress." We can multiply examples of these crowded recollections, sometimes accurate in all details, sometimes mistaken, as when he assures us he saw Fanny Wallack in *London Assurance* "as

Lady Gay Spanker, flushed and vociferous, first in a riding habit with a tail yards long and afterwards in yellow satin with scarce a tail at all." Fanny Wallack's last appearance in America was in June 1852 and *London Assurance* was not produced at Wallack's until 1854 with Rosa Bennett as Lady Gay. Henry may have been thinking of Miss Bennett as the lady with the long—and later abbreviated—train.

Dickens, next to Shakespeare, probably was the author who figured most frequently in Henry James's boyhood playgoing, although it is a question whether he figured more for him on the stage than in the book. The familiar characters were emerging freshly from magazine and volume and they were thrown hastily upon the stage by play tinkers seeking to give bodily form to the Micawbers and Scrooges, Pickwicks and Copperfields, Oliver Twists and Paul Dombeys, whose very names assured a full house. To Burton, Henry James was indebted for the Captain Cuttle of *Dombey and Son,* and he recalled him as a "monstrous Micawber . . . with the entire baldness of a huge easter egg and collar-points like the sails of Mediterranean feluccas." He must have seen him in that role, if not in 1850 when Burton gave *David Copperfield* at his theatre, then in the revivals of 1853 and 1855. At Burton's too he saw *Nicholas Nickleby* with Lizzie Weston as Smike "all tearful melodrama." In face of his recollection of these productions, the aged Henry mused, "who shall deny the immense authority of the theatre, or that the stage is the mightiest of modern engines? Such at least was to be the force of the Dickens imprint, however applied, in the soft clay of our generation; it was to resist so serenely the wash of the waves of time."

He saw one important drama that was to remain a landmark in the American theatre for successive generations. The Barnum version of *Uncle Tom's Cabin,* in which he had admired Emily Mestayer, was the third to reach the New York stage. Henry did not see the first, which had an abbreviated run at the National in 1852, and which the New York *Herald* reviewed indignantly with the question: "What will our southern friends think of all our professions of respect for their delicate social institution of slavery?" This production, without St. Clare, with no little Eva, no Topsy, and a spurious happy ending, came to its deserved close in two weeks. Eleven months later a full version by George L. Aiken, in six long acts, was brought out at the same theatre, eight tableaux and thirty scenes, embracing the whole of Mrs. Stowe's novel. It ran for three hundred performances (colored folk were allowed in the parquet for twenty-five cents through a special entrance). Impressed by this success Barnum produced the third version by H. J. Conway, with a happy ending. Undisturbed by competition, confident in his audiences, and particularly in the patronage of small boys at the matinees, he mounted it in November 1853 and here Henry saw it for the first time. In due course he saw the full-length production too, an evening particularly remembered, because it happened to be the occasion of his first theatre party and because he could be a "critic": he could compare the two versions. He was certain the second Eliza was less dramatic than Miss Mestayer; but the ice floes at the National did seem more genuine than the more obvious carpentry at Barnum's. And Henry James, writing of this evening at seventy, hints that it was all the richer for him in that its humor and pathos were collectively shared. He was absorbed as much by the junior audience as by the play. The little sophisticates had gone to *Uncle Tom* with some detachment, but found themselves swept along by the play's strong currents. It was initiation into social as well as aesthetic adventure.

### 3.

On June 27, 1855, the elder Henry sailed for Europe with his family to give his children "a better sensuous education than they were likely to get here." (Years later Henry, seeking perhaps to justify his long expatriation, carefully misquoted this remark, contained in a letter to Ralph Waldo Emerson, making it read "such a sensuous education as they can't get here.")

The initiation of the James boys into the European theatre was somewhat slower and less extensive than might have been expected of devoted young playgoers. Europe provided a drama richer than anything that could be found in the theatre, "life in general, all round us, was perceptibly more theatrical." There were other elements; the simple one of distance, for example. In New York the theatres had been within easy reach of Union Square. In London the distances to be traversed to the playhouses from St. John's Wood made theatregoing an elaborate and calculated ceremony. Henry James remembered "two throbbing and heaving cabs," travelling across vast, foggy tracts of the town, depositing the playgoers, after many twists and turns, before ancient theatres whose interiors seemed as labyrinthine as the trip to the West End. In Paris there was an additional limiting factor that had nothing to do with distance or the French language, which the boys had studied from an early age. The plays in the French capital were, as James put it, "out of relation to our time of life . . . our cultivated innocence." The plays in Manhattan had been directly addressed to such innocence in the adult audience, and hence were suited to children as well. This was, to a considerable degree, true also of London. The theatres of London offered in effect the same type of entertainment as those of New York—lurid melodrama and sprawling farce, sentimental drama and ranting eloquence, translations and bowdlerizations from the French. The acting was sometimes more finished; the diction may have been purer, but for the most part the plays of London were foreign counterparts of those seen in their native city.

London offered the excitement of the Christmas pantomime; it offered also Charles Mathews, Frederick Robson, Alfred Wigan and Charles Kean and the small boy saw them all. We have Henry's word for it that the "momentous" event in their London playgoing was Kean's production of *Henry VIII.* Kean played Wolsey, but the children were less conscious of the acting than of the elaborate spectacle, and notably Queen Katharine's dream-vision of beckoning and consoling angels which for weeks afterwards they tried to depict in water colors. "The spectacle had seemed to us prodigious—as it was doubtless at its time the last word of costly scenic science." (He was to see Kean again ten years later in Boston as Macbeth "without a rag of scenic reinforcement" and was struck by the fact that "no actor so little graced by nature probably ever went so far toward repairing it by a kind of cold rage of endeavor.")

Henry saw the stunted Robson, heard his hoarse voice, his grotesque delivery; Robson snarled and leered, he used to grind his teeth and roll his eyes, but he created vivid comedy and painful intensity. At the Olympic he saw Tom Taylor's *Still Waters Run Deep* with Wigan as John Mildmay; he saw Mathews in *The Critic* and a comedy "botched" from the French, *Married for Money.* He remembered nights at the Olympic in Wych Street, approached through the squalid slums—an "incredibly brutal and barbarous" avenue to an evening of theatrical joy.

They lingered a while in Paris. Here the staunch little playgoers were reduced to the level of circuses —the perpetual Cirque d'Été and the Cirque d'Hiver as well as the Théâtre du Cirque; nevertheless they relished the clowns and acrobats and the elaborate ballet-pantomime. Only two French plays were remembered from this time, played by Rose Chéri and Anaïs Fargueil. It seemed to him, in retrospect, that his boyhood stay in Paris was one of missed opportunities. It was the golden age of French acting. Rachel was dying, but her name was on everyone's lips. He did not see her. Neither did he see Déjazet, Mélingue or Samson. The memory of Mademoiselle Mars lingered; Mademoiselle Georges "a massive, a monstrous antique" had returned for a season. He missed her, as he missed the others.

He has recorded one missed opportunity in particular. "There emerges in my memory from the night of time the image of a small boy walking in the Palais-Royal with innocent American girls who were his cousins and wistfully hearing them relate how many times . . . they had seen Madame Doche in *La Dame aux Camélias* and what floods of tears she had made them weep." Charlotte Doche created the role of the unhappy Marguerite in 1852 and played it five hundred times; and for Henry James the name of Dumas *fils* could evoke distant memories: his wonder at the role his cousins gave the pocket handkerchief in the theatre; the manner in which his ears responded to the strange beauty of the title; the complete unawareness of the little girls—and Henry himself—of the social position of the lady of the expensive flowers.

4.

The small boy, an inveterate theatregoer, inevitably developed stage ambitions: he would be an actor; more important still, he would be a dramatist. His early experiences in stage production were confined, he recalled, to watching his older brother take charge of attic theatricals in which Albany cousins and playmates of the Fourteenth Street neighborhood participated. There was much more preparation than performance, "so much more conversation and costume than active rehearsal." William was in the thick of it all "throwing off into space conceptions that I could stare at across the interval but couldn't appropriate." William was producer, playwright and director rolled into one, while Henry stood in the "wings" bereft of garments, waiting for a costume, "unclad and impatient both as to our persons and to our aims, waiting alike for ideas and breeches."

There has survived, out of this time, a letter in its original rectangular envelope, postmarked Paris, but without legible date, addressed to "Master E. Van Winkle, 14 st. N. York" which attests to Henry's continued interest in neighborhood theatricals after the James family had taken up residence abroad. We can imagine the small boy, by then twelve or thirteen, sitting down in the Avenue Montaigne, in those early days of the Second Empire, to address this missive to far-away New York. The recipient was Edgar Van Winkle, who lived two doors away from the Jameses and for whom Henry had a deep respect ("Edgar walked in a maze of culture," Henry wrote decades later). It is the earliest letter of Henry James's to have survived. "Dear Eddy," it runs, with a brevity the novelist was seldom to achieve in his later correspondence, "As I heard you were going to try to turn the club

into a Theatre. And as I was asked w'ether I
wanted to belong here is my answer. I would like
very much to belong. Yours Truly H James."

His experiments in boyhood "play-writing" were
closely related to his brother's activities. William
James, at an early age, revealed a talent for drawing and devoted his young manhood to the study of
art. Henry, in emulation, also drew. He evokes for
us a picture of his older brother sitting in the evening under the lamplight sketching, with himself a
few feet away "engaged at that period . . . in literary—or to be more precise in dramatic, accompanied by pictorial composition . . . how could I
have doubted . . . with our large theatrical experience, of the nature, and of my understanding of the
dramatic form?" Is he trying not only to imitate
William, in brotherly rivalry, but to surpass him?
William, he explained, "drew because he could,
while I did so in the main only because he did."

At any rate he had evolved a ritual for these il-
lustrated dramas: quarto sheets were purchased in
a shop on Sixth Avenue, three sheets ruled, the
fourth unruled. The drama filled the ruled pages.
The blank page provided the space for the illustration. "I thought, I lisped, at any rate I composed
in scenes," he tells us in describing what he set
down on his quarto sheets. Every scene had its ex-
planatory picture and he strained toward the picture "which had . . . something of the interest of
the dramatist's casting of his *personae,* and must
have helped me to believe in the validity of my
subject."

"Picture" and "scene": the words were to figure
again and again in his critical writings. They became part of his special lexicon of critical terms
defining the arts of fiction and the drama as he
practised them. We are confronted in this instance,
as in others, with the question of how much of his

later art he read back into his childhood. The
novelist boasted that to the laying of a scene and
the launching of a drama he had always been faithful; and it would be entirely understandable that
in the circumstances he would think of himself as
having lisped and composed scenes at an early age.
We do know that during adolescence Henry was
"an immense writer of novels and dramas"; his father so described him in a letter from Boulogne.
His second son was not as fond of study "properly
so-called, as of reading." He was a "devourer of
libraries." The elder James added, in this letter,
written to Henry's grandmother, "he has considerable talent as a writer, but I am at a loss to know
whether he will ever accomplish much."

The "plays" written during this period by the
fourteen-year-old Henry perished long ago. However, a family anecdote throws light on their nature. Henry had drawn a picture of a mother and
child clinging to a rock in the midst of a stormy
ocean and had written underneath it: "The thunder roared and the lightning followed." William
James pounced upon the illustration. It is not in
the nature of older brothers to correct the mistakes
of their juniors with tact or indulgence. That
Henry should put thunder before lightning was a
meteorological blunder that invited high derision
from the scientifically-minded William. He tor-
mented the sensitive young writer to such an extent
that Henry promptly enacted part of his story. He
ran for maternal protection and invoked, and received, it for his quarto-sheet manuscript.

5.

Out of this childhood he recalled one particular
incident which, more than any other, illustrates his
sense of the Scene as well as of the Picture. His
father had taken him in the summer of 1854—when

he was eleven—on one of their rare visits to an
uncle's home, Linwood, at Rhinebeck on the Hudson. It was a broad, roomy estate. There were roses,
grapes, peaches, currant clusters, the hum of in-
sects, a wide view of the river with "great bright
harmonies of air and space." One evening the
eleven-year-old boy wandered to the eminence over-
looking the Hudson accompanied by his little cousin, Marie. She was of his age, small, brown, with
shining black eyes, and—he had been told—
"spoiled." That made her especially interesting,
since the James boys had never been "spoiled." It
gave her a romantic status to young Henry, who
only half understood the meaning of the term. His
uncle, Augustus James, sitting near by, remarked
with some emphasis that it was Marie's bedtime.
The words must have fallen with some weight; by
implication it was probably Henry's bedtime too.
What he remembered, however, half a century
later, was Marie's objection, a somewhat emphatic
rejoinder from Uncle Augustus, and Marie rushing
into her mother's arms "as if to a court of appeal."
From the aunt came simple words which appear to
have fallen with a sharp ring on the ears of the
small boy: "Come now, my dear; don't make a
scene—I *insist* on your not making a scene!"

"That was all the witchcraft the occasion used,"
wrote Henry, "but the note was none the less epoch-
making. The expression, so vivid, so portentous,
was one I had never heard—it had never been addressed to us at home; and who should say now
what a world one mightn't at once read into it? It
seemed freighted to sail so far; it told me so much
about life. Life at these intensities clearly became
'scenes'; but the great thing, the immense illumina-
tion, was that we could make them or not as we
chose."

It matters little the extent to which Henry James

read back into his reminiscent pages the implications of the incident in the light of his devotion to Picture and Scene. What is important is that he brought the incident out of the distant days of his childhood, to illuminate the course of his art. Henry James considered the episode a landmark in the history of his imagination.

## II. SCHOOL OF THE DRAMATIST

THE FATHER had sought a better "sensuous" education than he believed his sons could find in America. During their early European travels—between Henry's twelfth and seventeenth years, including a trip to America and a speedy return to Europe— the small boy was exposed to the rich panorama of the Old World: the London of Dickens and Thackeray, the Paris of the restored monarchy, the pensions and hotels of Switzerland, the provincial seaside life of Boulogne, and a brief glimpse of the stolid Germanic life of Bonn. The future novelist-dramatist was educated neither for the novel nor the drama; but he absorbed the materials for both in his reading of current literature, his nights at the play, his visits to art galleries, and his constant inspection of European architecture and landscape. The young Henry James who came back in 1859 to rediscover America from the pleasant perspective of Newport in Rhode Island, on the eve of the Civil War, had developed a sharpened vision of life and art, an international sense, an acute appreciation of Anglo-American culture and a good-humored understanding of the American abroad. He became a cosmopolitan without ever having been a provincial.

If this life contributed first and foremost to the creation of a great psychological novelist, it contained also those elements which contributed to his prolonged flirtation with the stage and the obsessive writings of his plays. He begins his career as a writer of fiction, but never without sidelong—and loving—glances at the theatre. In *A Small Boy* he injects the "note" of theatre recurrently: the memory of receiving Lamb's *Tales from Shakespeare* from a long-legged Scotsman who was his tutor in London and who later tutored Robert Louis Stevenson; schooldays at Boulogne with the pastry-cook's son, C. B. Coquelin, whom he was to admire on the stage of the Théâtre Français; a recollection of the way in which Monsieur Toeppfer, in Geneva, taught him Racine, describing Rachel's playing of Phèdre—her entrance "borne down, in her languorous passion, by the weight of her royal robes—*Que ces vains ornements, que ces voiles me pèsent!*—the long lapse of time before she spoke"; the memory of a night at the play in Bonn with his father (who in a letter has left us a record of his impression of Adelaide Ristori's portrayal on this occasion of *Maria Stuart*, "the vulture counterfeiting Jenny Wren. Every little while the hoarse, exulting voice, the sanguinary beak, the lurid bloated eye of menace, and the relentless talons, looked forth from the feathery mass and sickened you with disgust"). And the recollection of Frau Stromberg at Bonn, at whose pension William stayed, and who combined the art of making *Pfannkuchen* with dramaturgy, reading her five-act tragedy of *Cleopatra* to William and her other young boarders. He remembered the neat little volume and the fine print of the text which William borrowed for Henry to read. (Fifteen years later, in his story "Eugene Pickering," Henry attributed to his Germanic Madame Blumenthal the authorship of an *Historisches Trauerspiel* in fine print named *Cleopatra* in five acts.)

Elsewhere he has recorded a never-forgotten

image of Fanny Kemble (first glimpsed near New York when he was a little boy and she a celebrity riding on horseback), giving her readings from Shakespeare in assembly rooms in St. John's Wood, the great human thunder roll of the Kemble voice in *Lear,*

> *Howl, howl, howl, howl.*

He remembered the black velvet she wore on this occasion, the white satin in which she attired herself for a reading of *A Midsummer Night's Dream* and her "formidable splendor." The time was to come when Henry James would escort this formidable creature to the theatre and spend long London evenings at her fireside.

### 1.

He was seventeen and at Newport, walking along the moss-clad shore and over sand-starved grass to the Paradise Rocks, talking endlessly with John LaFarge and Thomas Sergeant Perry, reading Balzac and Merimée and the salmon-covered issues of the *Revue des Deux Mondes,* translating Alfred de Musset's *Lorenzaccio* into which, Perry has told us, "he introduced some scenes of his own." Henry James was to write tenderly of the Newport days and particularly of the hours spent with the young LaFarge, who encouraged him in his literary undertakings and introduced him to the poetry of Browning as well as to the French writers. It was essentially a period of initiation and discovery, of intensive reading, quiet cogitation and observation, tranquil literary labor.

The young man who turned up at the Harvard Law School at nineteen, during the second year of the Civil War, felt himself somewhat outside the society in which he lived. He was, moreover, as little interested in law as he had been in scientific studies attempted earlier at Geneva. William James had preceded him to Harvard and Henry, as in the past, gravitated in the same direction. The picture of the Harvard months, sketched in *Notes of a Son and Brother,* shows us a young man very much in search of himself. He went through the motions of trying for a legal "career," but he moved to one of his own choosing.

Of an evening he would journey into Boston by horse-car to see a play at the Howard Athenaeum. He found that the "half-buried Puritan curse" still lingered; he felt in the Bostonian attitude "that intimation more than anything else of the underhand snicker." He nevertheless went to the theatre as often as possible—despite the "implication of the provincial in the theatric air and of the rustic in the provincial." At seventy he pictured his student self—always with a touch of benign irony—as a critical and quite elevated young theatregoer, but he was little more sophisticated as an undergraduate than when he frequented Barnum's. He went to see Kate Bateman and he saw, and never forgot, the celebrated Maggie Mitchell in *Fanchon the Cricket,* translated from a German play by Augustus Wauldaur which in turn was derived from George Sand's *La Petite Fadette.* Miss Mitchell had played the one part up and down the United States ("she twanged that one string and none other, every night of her theatric life"). Yet there was nothing stale about the charm she exercised upon her youthful admirer. Henry returned entranced to his rooms in Winthrop Street and wrote her a letter "from which the admired Miss Maggie should gather the full force of my impression." This she seems to have done, for she reciprocated by autographing for him a printed "acting edition" of the play. The old man amusedly fancied his Harvard self as a dashing young Pendennis with Miss Mitchell as his Miss Fotheringay.

He recalled in particular, however, that the impression of the play and Miss Mitchell's acting prompted him to write an appreciation of the production and of the actress. "I first sat down beside my view of the Brighton hills to enrol myself in the bright band of the fondly hoping and fearfully doubting who count the days after the despatch of manuscripts." He adds coyly that "nothing would induce me now to name the periodical on whose protracted silence I had thus begun to hang." James's dramatic criticism never seems to have seen the light of print. But it is significant that the first bit of original writing he sent to a publication should have been devoted to an actress—and to a play.

2.

We have these anecdotes and incidents, the scattered clues to his reading, theatregoing, gallery-visiting, and yet little to explain the extraordinary maturity of his writing from the moment that he blossomed out at twenty-one in the pages of the *North American Review* and a few months later in the *Atlantic Monthly,* the newly-founded *Nation* and the *Galaxy.* Youthful the writing is, in its desire to be clever, to score points, to toss off neat epigrams, and in its dogmatism; yet as regards the fundamentals of art it possesses a distinct point of view, an individual terminology, a theory of fiction, of art, of drama that is vigorous and often original. One wonders where the school of the novelist and of the dramatist had been. How could so desultory an education have produced so balanced and coherent a practitioner of the art of writing? The answer lies deeply embedded in the whole history of James's imaginative and emotional education, in his boyhood years of observing and reading, and in those tensions which he discovered his pen could ease—and use.* Henry James was to develop during the next half-century a much more complex aesthetic; he was to develop a style, a manner, an elaborate doctrine relating to fiction and the scenic art: yet from the first he knew what he wanted to do, and how to go about doing it. So much *savoir-faire* in one so young could only be explained in the facts that James himself adduced in his autobiographies: his was the history and growth of a curious, observing, retaining and disciplined mind, stimulated and sharpened in the family circle, and flourishing in spite of repeated attempts to regiment it within the framework of "education." The anonymous reviewer in the *Nation* who accorded an extended article to James's first volume of short stories on June 24, 1875, when the novelist was thirty-two, had a valid, if elaborate, explanation: "He has seen more cities and manners of man than was possible in the slower days of Ulysses, and if with less gain of worldly wisdom, yet with an enlargement of his artistic apprehensiveness and scope that is of far greater value to him." His *artistic apprehensiveness*—this, perhaps, is as good a term as we could wish to describe the primary source of James's creativity.

During the first ten years of his creative life, James established himself as a literary critic, a writer of travel pieces, a master of the short story and—at the end of the decade—as a novelist. From 1865, when his critical articles began to appear in ever-increasing numbers, to the end of 1875, the year in which he took up permanent residence abroad, he wrote 26 short stories, 132 book reviews,

* I have sought to describe this process in greater detail in my life of Henry James, *The Untried Years: 1843-1870.*

43 travel articles, 10 papers devoted to art criticism, seven articles on the drama, three dramatic sketches or comediettas and two novels in serial form. Much of the material for this work was the fruit of his absorption of American life in Boston and New York; most of it stemmed from two trips abroad during 1869-70 and 1872-74; all of it went back to roots buried deeply during the years of his "sensuous" education.

If at the end of this crowded decade of travel, discovery, creation, Henry James emerged as a full-fledged novelist, he emerged also with a full-fledged theory of the drama. It might be observed that he developed as well his critical notation of painting and that the plastic arts loomed much larger in the work of these years than did the theatre. These were the years of his discovery of Italy and the glories of its art; his enthusiasm for painting and architecture overflowed into his travel sketches and his stories. Painting attracted him as a fictional subject. But the fascination of the drama was something deeper. Play-writing was a craft allied to fiction. Henry James never tried to paint pictures, once he discarded the drawing pencil and brush at Newport. But he *did* write plays. The dramatist existed within the novelist: both might look upon art with an appraising and critical eye—but each had a separate creative task to perform.

He held "dramatic interest" essential to good novel-writing. Give me "dramatic compactness," he lectured George Eliot, in his review of *Felix Holt,* criticizing her for creating "intense" characters without showing them in action. Miss Alcott's *Moods* provoked him to suggest that she was insufficiently acquainted with people "to handle great dramatic passions." As a consequence, he observed, discussing her novel as if it were a drama, "her play is not a real play, nor her actors real actors." Reviewing Miss Braddon's *Aurora Floyd* he speaks of play-writing as "an arduous profession"—as if at twenty-two he had already tried his hand at it and found the going difficult.

Of Swinburne's *Chastelard,* in the *Nation* (January 18, 1866) he remarks at twenty-three with the assurance of his years, "it is comparatively easy to write energetic poetry, but . . . it is very difficult to write a good play." He tells Swinburne: "You have to have more than a pretty idea to carry a play." He tells him again: "A dramatic work without design is a monstrosity." He offers him advice: "Chastelard descants in twenty different passages of very florid and eloquent verse upon the intoxicating beauties of his mistress; but meanwhile the play stands still . . . let him talk as much as he pleases, and let him deal out poetry by the handful, the more the better. But meanwhile let not the play languish, let not the story halt."

He had, thus, a decidedly "fixed" view of what drama, action, scene should be, and during the ten years that followed his first appearance in print he was to develop a consistent—and quite dogmatic—conception of what acting and production should be in the theatre itself. The young writer who left Cambridge in 1869 at twenty-six on his first adult journey abroad was to spend many nights in the playhouses of Europe. In strange cities, with long evenings before him, he gravitated toward the theatre arguing that here he would find a reflection of the civilization he was visiting, that a country's culture can be studied at first hand in the plays it mounts and in the audiences that come to see them.

Henry James paid his first visits to the Théâtre Français and the theatres of the Paris boulevards during 1870, regretting that he could not tarry longer, asserting emphatically in due course that the French national theatre constituted a school of

taste "not elsewhere to be found in the world."
During 1872-73 we can follow him from France into
Italy. He pauses for a week at Perugia and goes to
the theatre nightly, paying twenty-two soldi for an
orchestra seat, seeing such plays as *Amore Senza
Stima, Severità e Debolezza, La Società Equivoca,*
feeling that his study of the audiences brings him
close to the people of the Italian town. We catch
him in Rome at the Teatro Valle listening to
Goldoni's *I Quattro Rustighi* done in the Venetian
dialect which he can only half follow: the acting
not as fine as the French, but "in some of the
women—ugly, with red hands and shabby dresses—
an extraordinary gift of natural utterance, of seem-
ing to invent joyously as they go." And we find him
that same month in a box at the Apollo, in Rome,
surveying Italian princesses in neighboring boxes
and watching a violent Othello played by Ernesto
Rossi. Othello seized Iago, whacked his head "half
a dozen times on the floor" and then flung him
"twenty yards away." Wonderfully done, observed
the young American, but "in the doing of it, and
in the evident relish for it in the house there was I
scarce know what force of easy and thereby rather
cheap expression."

### 3.

Early in 1875, while Henry James's first long
novel was appearing in the *Atlantic Monthly,* he
went to New York for a few months and served as
a casual critic for the *Nation,* reviewing art shows
and plays. He saw Ristori and Rignold, *The Two
Orphans* and a play entitled *Women of the Day*
which he described as an "unqualifiable mess of
vulgarity . . . ghastly, monstrous, a positive nightmare." He had little good to say of the New York
season, and before the year was out he had decided
to take up permanent residence in Europe. Before

sailing he gave fullest expression to his theory of the drama, not in any formalized manner, but in a long review of Tennyson's *Queen Mary* written for the *Galaxy,* and published in September 1875. He was to repeat and amplify these views, even as he had forecast them in his dramatic criticism, but he was never to alter them. As late as 1908 they are re-expressed in his prefaces.

"The dramatic form," he wrote in the review, "seems to me of all literary forms the noblest," and he added promptly this personal note: "I have so extreme a relish for it that I am half afraid to trust myself to praise it, lest I should seem to be merely rhapsodizing. But to be really noble it must be quite itself. . . ." And he goes on:

The fine thing in a real drama, generally speaking, is that, more than any other work of literary art, it needs a masterly structure. It needs to be shaped and fashioned and laid together, and this process makes a demand upon an artist's rarest gifts. He must combine and arrange, interpolate and eliminate, play the joiner with the most attentive skill; and yet at the end effectually bury his tools and his sawdust, and invest his elaborate skeleton with the smoothest and most polished integument. The five-act drama—serious or humorous, poetic or prosaic—is like a box of fixed dimensions and inelastic material, into which a mass of precious things are to be packed away. It is a problem in ingenuity and a problem of the most interesting kind. The precious things in question seem out of all proportion to the compass of the receptacle; but the artist has an assurance that with patience and skill a place may be made for each, and that nothing need be clipped or crumpled, squeezed or damaged. The false dramatist either knocks out the sides of his box, or plays the deuce with the contents; the real one gets down on his knees, disposes of his goods tentatively, this, that, and the other way, loses his temper but keeps his ideal, and at last rises in triumph, having packed his coffer in the one way that is mathematically right. It closes perfectly, and the lock turns with a click; between one object and another you cannot insert the point of a penknife.

To work successfully beneath a few grave, rigid laws, is always a strong man's highest ideal of success . . . In a play, certainly, the subject is of more importance than in any other work of art. Infelicity, triviality, vagueness of subject, may be outweighed in a poem, a novel, or a picture, by charm of manner, by ingenuity of execution; but in a drama the subject is of the essence of the work—it *is* the work. If it is feeble, the work can have no force; if it is shapeless, the work must be amorphous.

An important subject, moulded by "a few grave, rigid laws"—this, then, was Henry James's recipe for a good play, and few persons can quarrel with such a classical formulation. He is asking for perfection of form and content and a goodly measure of each, harmoniously wedded. What stands out, however, is his insistence upon "grave and rigid" laws. We may find it difficult, in the light of the greater scenic fluidity of our theatre and the influence of the cinema, to accept so chaste a definition. For James, in his time, confronted with the anarchy of the Anglo-American stage and the neatness and precision of the French—and given his fastidious personality and his delight in a disciplined and ordered art—there seemed to be no choice. He accepted the "laws" of the theatre of which Francisque Sarcey in Paris was the principal critical exponent: a play had to be "well-made" and this meant flawless "technique." He upheld the French classical theory of the drama, but applied it to the melodramatic, manipulated dramas of Scribe and Sardou. When Henry James, making his start as a playwright, exclaimed, *"À moi, Scribe, à moi, Sardou, à moi, Dennery!"* he was invoking the dramatists who were the special gods of Francisque Sarcey. A brilliant and documented critic, Sarcey nevertheless had one set of laws for all times and all dramatists. For James he was "inimitable and incorruptible." James saw him as one who believed in the theatre as if it were a religion and loved it with an abiding passion. From Sarcey's writings James derived much of his knowledge of the French stage of the time and of its immediate past, and an excess of theory to match his own observations of the Maison de Molière in the rue de Richelieu.

4.

When Hyacinth Robinson, in *The Princess Casamassima,* took Millicent Henning to a London theatre to see *The Pearl of Paraguay,* "his imagination projected itself lovingly across the footlights, gilded and colored the shabby canvas and battered accessories, losing itself so effectually in the fictive world that the end of the piece, however long or however short, brought with it something of the alarm of a stoppage of his personal life. It was impossible to be more friendly to the dramatic illusion."

In attributing what he also called the "dear old playhouse spell" to his hero, Henry James endowed him with his own deeply subjective attitude toward the stage. For James's creative imagination could not but ally itself with the stage's "fictive world," and the end of a play for him would indeed be the stoppage of his "personal life." Henry James has told us how in going to the Théâtre Français he found "an ideal and exemplary world," a "world that has managed to attain all the felicities that the world we live in misses."

What were these felicities and what was this world? Henry James describes it: it is smooth, harmonious, artistic. Great attention is paid to detail.

The people do the things "that we should like to
do; they are gifted as we should like to be; they
have mastered the accomplishments that we have
had to give up." The women are not all beautiful
but they are graceful, agreeable, sympathetic, "lady-
like," perfectly dressed, possessed of the best manners, charming, with musical voices. They speak
with "irreproachable purity and sweetness." They
walk with elegant grace. In short, they are the Milly
Theales, Isabel Archers, Mme. de Cintrés and Maggie Ververs of James's fiction.

And the men? They were not handsome either
(except Mounet-Sully who was an "Adonis of the
first magnitude") but they looked whatever part
they played; they were as well-mannered and as
agreeably spoken as the ladies. "They represent
gentlemen, and they produce the illusion." Emotion and passion were controlled, parcelled out in
scenes and acts, with appropriate well-timed cli-
maxes. For the "visual" Henry James, the "individual so capable as I am of the uncanniest self-efface-
ment in the active exercise of the passion of
observation" as he described himself, here was a
way to look actively at life recreated, while main-
taining a state of sublime passivity. Henry James
could sit quietly yet nothing was lost upon him.
This was perfection indeed: an ordered world
played out on a large and beautiful stage and with
an art as consummate as that which he lavished
upon his own work.

The Théâtre Français was steeped in the past; it
had traditions and standards, rituals and observ-
ances. No dinner could be too hastily swallowed in
order to be at the seven o'clock curtain, to see such
actresses as Madame Nathalie in Feuillet's *Le Village;* no uncomfortable stall could diminish the
dazzling qualities of Favart and Croizette, Brohan
and Bressart, Regnier and Got, Mounet-Sully and

Coquelin; no "pestilential" atmosphere—meaning quite simply the theatre's poor ventilation—could spoil the magic sense that in the air of the building, in the dim reaches of the great dome, there slept the echoes of Rachel's voice, the sense that these footlights had illuminated the tragedienne's finest moments. Herr Toeppfer had described this during the novelist's student days at Geneva; now Henry James could discover it for himself.

He saw his first performance in the rue de Richelieu on the eve of the Franco-Prussian war— Augier's *Lions et Renards* with Coquelin or *L'Aventurière,* we cannot be sure which of the two it was. He was in the capital again two years later in the wake of the Commune, visiting the barricades; he spoke of there being still the smell of blood and of gunpowder in the air; and he went "every night— or almost" to the Théâtre Français. On Sunday evenings he would dine with James Russell Lowell at his hotel on the Left Bank near the Chamber of Deputies and, he wrote later, "I never cross the Seine amid the wet flare of the myriad lamps, never note the varnished rush of the river or the way the Louvre grows superb in the darkness without a recurrent consciousness of the old sociable errand, the sense of dipping into a still denser Paris with the *Temps* and M. Sarcey in my pocket." Lowell and Sarcey were James's mentors during this Parisian sojourn in which the Théâtre Français assumed an importance for him that was never to be erased.

There were two nights which stood out in memory, both of a later date, the autumn of 1877. On one of these he saw Dumas the Younger's *Le Demi-Monde* which inspired his *Siege of London;* on the other he saw a play by Charles Lomon, *Jean Dacier,* with Coquelin. He later described how he left the theatre "agitated" with what he had seen, pacing

the streets far into the night, wanting to write plays
for such actors, carried away by the spell they had
exercised. He quarreled with the plot of *Le Demi-
Monde,* he thought *Jean Dacier* weak as a play, but
he was nevertheless stimulated and inspired by the
art with which they had been done. "Far away and
unspeakably regretted the days, alas, or, more exactly the nights, on which one could walk away
from the Français under the spell of such fond con-
victions and such deep and agitating problems," he
wrote thirty years after that Paris autumn.

To Benoît Constant Coquelin Henry James's
most vivid impressions of the French stage attached
themselves: "the rich, the rare, the admirable and
inimitable" Coquelin, the "most joyous and exuber-
ant of pure comedians." They had been to school
together as boys at the Collège Communal in Boulogne, and to these memories of childhood was now
added the excitement of seeing a mature and accomplished artist. He remembered how, on leaving the theatre after *Jean Dacier,* "I walked about
a long time under the influence not so much of the
piece as of Coquelin's acting of it, which had made
the thing so human, so brilliant, so valuable. I was
agitated with what it said to me that I might do—
what I ought to attempt."

This was nothing compared to "the state I was
thrown into by meeting Coquelin." He met him at
Andrew Lang's in 1879 when the Comédie Fran-
çaise came to London. Henry wrote that "it stirred
me to the depths. . . . It excited me powerfully,"
the way in which Coquelin's personality overflowed
into his talk. "All day, and for days afterward, I
remained under the impression." In his journal he
referred to the two Coquelin episodes (one of which
he embodied later in a long essay on Coquelin published in 1887 and revised just before his death) as

"landmarks" in the history of his theatrical ambitions.

These constituted the final steps in Henry James's education for the theatre. He had assimilated French dramatic theory and he found himself on terms of growing intimacy with some of the players. Coquelin came to lunch, and later wrote to him encouragingly from Paris urging him on in his dramatic ambitions. When are you being acted? Coquelin queried, and he added that James had only to give him a signal and he would come to see him played.

5.

James devoted nine essays and reviews to the French stage. His best-known is the urbane essay he contributed to the *Galaxy* (and included in *French Poets and Novelists*) which summed up his impressions of the Théâtre Français. Shortly after settling in London, in 1877, he did the same for the London theatres. He found British audiences less Bohemian, less blasé, more naïf, "well dressed, tranquil, motionless" suggesting domestic virtue and comfortable homes. The British audience looked to him as if it had come to the play in its own carriage, after a dinner of beef and pudding. The ladies "are mild, fresh-colored English mothers. . . . There are many rosy young girls, with dull eyes and quiet cheeks—an element wholly absent from Paris audiences. The men are handsome and honorable-looking. . . . Altogether they are much more the sort of people to spend a quiet evening with than the clever, cynical, democratic multitude that surges nightly out of the brilliant Boulevards into those temples in which MM. Dumas *fils* and Sardou are the high priests. But," added James, "you might spend your evening with them better almost anywhere than at the theatre."

He was to live the rest of his life among the people he thus described and he was to attempt to write plays for them. "The art of writing a play has apparently become a lost one with the English race," he wrote, and set about planning to revive this art. "There can be no serious school of acting unless there is a dramatic literature to feed it," and he believed himself capable of creating such a literature. He was unsparing in his criticism of British plays and British acting. For him the French theatre remained the one theatre worthy of emulation. "The French esteem the theatre too much to take rash liberties with it," he wrote attacking the British theatre for its meagreness, its scenic excesses, its "barbarism." One of these liberties was the way in which it adapted plays from the French: "An English arrangement of a French piece is a pretty woman with her back turned."

The nights in the rue de Richelieu colored his view of the London stage and they were the "light by which one must work" for the theatre. To his journal, in 1881, the novelist confided: "The French stage I have mastered; I say that without hesitation. I have it in my pocket. . . . I have laid up treasures of wisdom. . . ." To William James he had written four years earlier: "My inspection of the French theatre will fructify. I have thoroughly mastered Dumas, Augier and Sardou . . . and I know all they know and a great deal more besides."

What did Henry James mean when he boasted that he had the French theatre "in my pocket"? He had studied it with all the earnestness and solemnity of a college student, methodically reading texts and going to see them acted. He had read the critics. He had, moreover, watched the actors. If he wrote of the plays as a literary critic, and complained that French playwrights contrived only endless variations on the theme of adultery, he wrote of the actors as if he were a professional man of the theatre, a stage director, a producer. In the history of dramatic criticism there are few writers who described scenery and costumes as closely and who dwelt in such detail on the histrionic technique. Like Sarcey, James cultivated the theatrical eye. The manner in which an actor walks is important to him; he pays close attention to his diction; he observes that the trivial act of taking a letter from a servant or placing a hat upon a chair can be made suggestive and interesting. He talks as if he had attended the *Conservatoire*. He not only has advice for the players; he considers himself qualified to go beyond Prince Hamlet, to step upon the stage and coach them—which is what he ultimately did.

The extent to which he had steeped himself in the practical side of production is revealed to us in his long novel of the stage, *The Tragic Muse,* which he completed just before beginning his play-writing. In those portions of the novel which are devoted to the career of Miriam Rooth—a fictional English counterpart to Rachel or Sarah Bernhardt —he not only echoes the lessons of the rue de Richelieu and his dramatic theory (as well as his sense that actors, self-absorbed and exhibitionistic, can have their life only on the stage), but reveals in the process intimate knowledge of the Théâtre Français backstage as well as front. One of the great scenes in the novel, inspired by a visit James paid to the *loge* of Julia Bartet when she was appearing in *L'École des Maris* in January 1889, describes the green room, the actors behind scenes, the corridors, the portraits, and the personality of a French actress such as Bartet.

His feelings about the Théâtre Français are

echoed from page to page in the novel. One character ventures to suggest that it is a greater institution than the House of Commons; Madame Carré, the retired French actress, who might have been drawn out of Fanny Kemble, observes, with the delightful French insularity which James understood, *"Je ne connais qu'une scène—la nôtre,"* a view James held to be the truth; and Gabriel Nash, the character in the novel who speaks for—and even resembles physically—the novelist himself, says, "The theatre in our country is puerile and barbarous." When Mrs. Rooth, Miriam's mother, observes that she wouldn't want her daughter to play a bad woman, Madame Carré rejoins: "Ah, in England then, and in your theatre, everyone's immaculately good? Your plays must be even more ingenious than I supposed!" And Gabriel Nash-James comes in, a solemn chorus: "We haven't any plays." Miriam says she wants to play Shakespeare, and Madame Carré wryly observes this is fortunate "as in English you haven't anyone else to play."

Thus the nights in the rue de Richelieu overflowed into his writings. "To be read 200 years after your death," he wrote, "is something, but to be acted is better."

And yet the years passed, and he did not write plays.

## III. APOLOGIES FOR THE THEATRE

THE YEARS passed but he wrote no plays. His theatrical ship had taken aboard a cargo of experience; its hold bulged with elaborate, heavily-documented dramatic theory, enough playgoing to crowd a lifetime, the memory of performances and performers in many playhouses in many lands. And still the ship did not set sail. At thirty-three he had

written to William James: "I know the Théâtre
Français by heart." At thirty-five he wrote to him:
"It has long been my most earnest and definite
intention to commence at play-writing as soon as I
can. . . ." And again during the same year: "I am
very impatient to get at work writing for the
stage—a project I have long had. I am . . . certain
I should succeed and it would be an open gate to
money-making." And now he was approaching forty
—and still the ship had not set sail.

For a man "impatient" to get at play-writing, he
was procrastinating to an extraordinary degree. He
had written three little closet dramas, chamber
plays or comediettas, one when he was twenty-six,
and two at twenty-nine, brief experiments in dialogue, but these were not serious efforts, certainly
not intended for the theatre. Between his thirtieth
and fortieth years he had published three major
novels and many short stories; innumerable critical
and travel articles. He had a fast-moving pen, and
a stream of work left his desk wherever he might be
—in England, France or Italy. Yet something was
keeping him back from the drama, and one day the
question rose to the surface of his mind and crept
out of the tip of the pen into the pages of his
journal.

It was on December 26, 1881. He had returned
to America after an absence of six years. He was in
Cambridge and he was taking a sheet of paper into
his confidence. He had talked with the owners of
the new Madison Square Theatre in New York, the
brothers Mallory, both clergymen, and their manager, Daniel Frohman. They had invited him to
dramatize his highly-successful short story, "Daisy
Miller." He wrote in his journal: "After long years
of waiting, of obstruction, I find myself able to put
into execution the most cherished of all my projects
—that of beginning to work for the stage. It was

one of my earliest—I had it from the first. None has given me brighter hopes—none has given me sweeter emotions." And then, in a moment of self-questioning, he adds: "It is strange nevertheless that I should never have done anything—and to a certain extent it is ominous. I wonder at times that the dream should not have faded away."

### 1.

It was strange and it was ominous. What follows in his journal is an illuminating passage of self-examination on the one hand and heavy rationalization on the other. He told himself that that there were good reasons for his failure to write plays—because of the "little work at any time that I could do," because he had needed "money on the spot" and this his fiction had provided; because of his "inability to do two things at once," and the "absence of opportunities, of openings." He could afford to wait, he told himself, since the drama was the ripest of the arts and "while I was waiting I was studying. . . ." James wrote that he was reminding himself of these "obstacles" to "justify my innumerable postponements."

Yet he had not quite convinced himself. He went on to hammer home these arguments, underscoring words as he wrote: ". . . it seems to me simply deplorable that I should not have got at work before. *But it was impossible at the time,* and I knew my chance would come." This need for self-justification can be understood readily. The arguments he gave himself were not altogether valid.

He complained of the little work he could do at any time, and indeed he made that complaint often; yet judged by any standards of literary productivity he had accomplished a lifetime of work when he wrote these words. During eighteen years of writing he had published fifteen volumes—fiction, travel, short stories; his novels included, by this time, *Roderick Hudson, The American, The Portrait of a Lady, Washington Square* and such diverse tales as "The Madonna of the Future" and "Daisy Miller." He had written articles and reviews in the *North American Review,* the *Galaxy,* the *Atlantic Monthly;* he had been correspondent of the New York *Tribune* and the *Nation.* It was true that he always felt that he could have produced more; but it was equally true that so active a pen could have attempted the plays Henry James kept saying he wanted to write.

The need for "money on the spot"? To a certain extent this was true: by keeping his literary pot boiling—and he regarded many of his works as "potboilers"—he was able to live comfortably and, because his needs were modest, create a margin of security for himself. At this particular time, he was receiving substantial sums from two sources for the simultaneous serialization of *The Portrait of a Lady* in *Macmillan's* in England and the *Atlantic Monthly* in the United States—not to speak of additional earnings from fugitive writing. This does not alter the fact of his feeling of insecurity; even larger earnings would have seemed to him insufficient.

"Inability to do two things at once"? He was doing just that constantly: delivering his monthly instalment of his current novel and at the same time producing short stories and articles. As index of his capacity to juggle a number of literary commitments simultaneously we may cite his work for 1879, the year of his greatest success which attended publication of his tale, "Daisy Miller"; he saw the tale through the press in book form, and published also his study of Hawthorne, a two-volume collection of short stories, carefully revised in their transference from magazine to book (*The Madonna of the*

*Future and Other Tales*), all this while feeding his serial *Confidence* to *Scribner's,* and writing three short stories, nine articles in the *Nation,* one for *Lippincott's* and one in the *North American Review.* Nevertheless on this score we must remember that play-writing has more often than not been considered an effort alien to a novelist; James might have been capable of writing several things simultaneously and would still consider the writing of a play at the same time the doing of "two things at once."

"Absence of opportunities"? In the very journal entry in which he speaks of this, he mentions that John Hare, one of London's leading actor-managers, had asked him to write a play and "offered me his services in the event of my doing so." James knew very well that a playwright need not wait for opportunities to market his work any more than a writer of fiction. He submitted his articles and short stories to editors; he could have submitted his plays just as well to managers. He had, however, been singularly fortunate in his literary opportunities; Charles Eliot Norton, William Dean Howells and James Russell Lowell had opened doors for him, recognizing at once his extraordinary talents. For one of his nature, however, the thought of having to push doors open himself in the theatre might be considered an "absence of opportunity."

Deeper reasons than those he gave must have kept him from writing the plays he wanted to write: fear of turning aside from familiar places of publication; hesitation to embark on the practical hazards of the theatre. The contempt he expressed so often for these hazards was alone a symptom of his anxiety. Publishers sought out Henry James during those years—theatre managers and actors merely evinced an interest in a possibly "useable" script. In his study he could write as he wished, fol-

low the high demands of "art" in accordance with
his own standards and principles and the public
could take him—or leave him. "One must go one's
way and know what one's about and have a general
plan and a private religion—in short have made up
one's mind as to *ce qui en est* with a public the
draggling after which simply leads one in the gutter.
One has always a 'public' enough if one has an
audible vibration—even if it should only come from
one's self." He put it thus to his brother on the eve
of his dramatic years. To venture into the theatre
was to forsake this "private religion"; it involved
obtaining approval of one's creations from men with
a greater concern for the pocketbook than for
"audible vibration"—except as the vibration meant
box office returns; of actors interested in the work
largely as a vehicle for exhibiting their own talents;
and finally it involved a search for the approval of
a heterogeneous public for which one had to dot
one's i's with pumpkins—an image he used later in
describing the simplicity of statement to which he
felt the drama reduced him. The reticent, secretive,
aloof literary alchemist of Bolton Street and De
Vere Gardens, a feted London "lion" moving in the
world as a conscious observer and recorder, rebelled
at the very things which are the life of the stage.
If he could have become a dramatist as he had become a man of letters he would have long before
turned to play-writing. As it was, he found himself
of two minds about the theatre. This led to in-
action.

He was attracted to the theatre and at the same
time was repelled by it. He wanted its successes
and rewards and yet was afraid to chance its pit-
falls. A work of fiction might receive adverse reviews
and fall flat in the market and still remain an hon-
orable performance; it did not involve the public
*exposure* that went with a play. When a magazine

rejected a story—this was a private matter between editor and writer. But when a play was announced, publicized, promised to the public, and then not produced, or failed in production, the author was, in the process, publicly rejected. This was what Henry James feared more than anything else.

He was not alone in his creative problem. A long line of literary men had sought, long before him, to be playwrights, with varying conflicts and varying success. In his own century Byron had faced the drama with a loathing akin to Henry James's. Tennyson had ventured into it late in life, carried by the tide of his poetic and public stature; Meredith had secretly attempted to write a play, but it had never left his desk; Thomas Hardy dramatized one of his tales, and later wrote *The Dynasts* without regard for the "laws" of the drama; George Moore joined his fellow writers of Ireland in a serious involvement with the stage; Swinburne had written long poetic dramas which the younger James had tartly reviewed. Henry James's Continental models, Balzac and Turgenev, had written plays without notable success. There was ample precedent for James among the men of literature, so that he might have faced his own attempts with equanimity. For him, however, the theatre became the focus of anxiety and conflicting emotions that caused him to approach it with faltering footsteps.

His dramatization of *Daisy Miller* in 1882 was turned down by the Madison Square Theatre and, promptly discouraged, Henry James returned to the writing of fiction. During the next six years he wrote his three large novels of the 1880's—*The Bostonians, The Princess Casamassima* and *The Tragic Muse*. He published the play version of *Daisy* in 1883 and the following year turned down a proposal that he dramatize *The Portrait of a Lady,* writing to the actor Lawrence Barrett, who suggested it, that he could not envision it as a play. Nevertheless he told him "I should be glad to try something next year. . . . I should probably be prepared to write you a play, to take or to leave, as you should like it or not, on the chance that if you *should* like it, it would open the door to my acquiring a goodish sum of money."

He was not, however, free for a sustained dramatic effort. His big novels, all serialized, kept him constantly at his desk. In 1886 he told one correspondent (Julian R. Sturgis) that he was not interested in trying to write plays because of "the whole general disillusionment that has come over me. . . . When I was younger that was really a very dear dream with me—but it has faded away with the mere increase of observation—observation I mean, of the deadly vulgarity and illiteracy of the world one enters, practically, in knocking at a manager's door. Besides I think, I confess, less highly of the drama, as a form, a vehicle, than I did—compared with the novel which can do and say so much more."

Three years later he was expressing the opposite view; and for one claiming a waning interest in the drama he applied himself to its problems assiduously even if he wrote no plays. When he wrote this letter he was already planning his long novel of the stage, *The Tragic Muse*.

2.

At forty Henry James had sought to convince himself that he should write plays. At the threshold of fifty he turned to the theatre in desperation. "My books don't sell, and it looks as if my plays might." This was the rueful confession he made to Robert Louis Stevenson in 1891.

For the Henry James of the impressive beard and the calm eye found himself, in the late Victorian

London, in the anomalous position of being a literary lion whose works were little read. He had caught the public fancy with his "international" tales, and notably "Daisy Miller," but the success had been short-lived. Within a decade James had found a public and lost it. Or had the public lost him? Publishers still brought him out, because it continued to be an honor to have him on their lists. The pages of the *Atlantic* continued to be open to him, and now and again one of his shorter pieces created a mild flurry. The golden moment of "success," nevertheless, seemed to have come and gone forever. "I have entered upon evil days," James wrote to Howells, who had been his mentor and companion in the early Cambridge time and to whom he turned constantly for practical advice about the marketing of his work. "I am still staggering a good deal under the mysterious and (to me) inexplicable injury wrought—apparently— upon my situation by my last two novels, the *Bostonians* and the *Princess*. They have reduced the desire, and the demand, for my productions, to zero."

It is always rather risky for a writer concerned with the marketplace of letters, to shift too far from the subject which has endeared him to his audience: the audience may not shift with him. This is what happened to Henry James. His readers were expecting an unending supply of stories about American girls and their adventures in Europe. Instead they got three massive "social" novels. Widely different in substance, *The Bostonians, The Princess Casamassima* and *The Tragic Muse* were in reality variations on a single theme. Reduced to their essence, they give us a glimpse into Henry James's problems. *The Bostonians* is the story of Verena Tarrant, a girl with a gift for platform oratory—hence an actress-type. She becomes the centre of a struggle between a domineering Boston suffragette who "uses" her to live out her own frustrated will to power, and a gentle anti-feminist Southerner, who invites her to abandon public life and to marry him. This happens also in a different way to the actress Miriam Rooth, in *The Tragic Muse:* in both cases James is dealing with the private life of a public woman. But *The Bostonians* also offers a large picture of New England "reformers." And in *The Princess Casamassima* James deals with a more violent kind of reform—the bomb-throwing anarchists of the 1880's, who wished to overthrow the social order. Hyacinth Robinson, James's young London hero, commits himself to revolution, but when the time comes he realizes that he likes the *status quo* too much to want to change it. *The Tragic Muse* contains within it a political theme as well as a stage theme; young Nick Dormer, a counterpart to Hyacinth, is pushed into politics by overwhelming family pressure, although he would much prefer to be a painter. The common denominator of the three novels is that of the coercion of the individual, and the artist, into forms of action alien to himself. James seems to be saying that society would like to destroy or "use" artists because they refuse to conform to the rules of the philistines; and that the artist, who by his very nature is a rebel, must protect himself even at the risk of being destroyed by his own rebellion. However, an artist such as James also is devoted to the society which nourishes him. He is not, like Joyce, wholly alienated from it. His dilemma therefore is that he finds himself wanting to defy the very order to which he is attached.

This was the essence of James's problem. Like his heroines in these novels he possessed a particular art; but his public—his readers, his publishers— wanted to "use" him, to coerce him into creating things which went against the grain of his artist-nature. Like his heroes he would have liked to defy the philistine world, blow it up, like the anarchists, and go his own way. But to blow it up would be to destroy his own world as well. On the deeper levels of feeling he was perhaps repeating old patterns of childhood: the competition with his brothers for parental acceptance, approval and love which James won not by defiance but by indirection and verbal skill. It is by some such process that he found himself gravitating toward the theatre: if the world did not want his novels (or wanted the kind of writing he did not want to do), perhaps it would pay cash at the box office, or applaud his plays—and by this ready means give him the freedom he needed as artist and as man. Thus began his "dramatic years." They were to prove sufficiently dramatic before they came to an end.

### 3.

He was in Paris in December 1888, freshly come from a stay in Geneva, and a trip to the Riviera, when the offer came: a suggestion by Edward Compton, a young actor-manager, whose company's activities were confined to the British provinces, to dramatize *The American*. Compton's wife, the American actress Virginia Bateman, had read an article in a theatrical publication suggesting that James's 1877 novel was a good subject for a play. Compton's proposal came at a good moment; this was the year during which James was acutely aware of his waning literary fortunes. It found him also at work on *The Tragic Muse* which he had begun that summer. In a journal note of May 12, 1889, when he was completing the *Muse,* he takes up again the self-examination, on the subject of the drama, of eight years earlier:

I had practically given up my old, valued, long cherished dream of doing something for the stage, for fame's sake, and art's, and fortune's: overcome by the vulgarity, the brutality, the baseness of the condition of the English-speaking theatre today. But after an interval, a long one, the vision has revived, on a new and a very much humbler basis, and especially under the lash of necessity. Of art or fame *il est maintenant fort peu question:* I simply *must* try, and try seriously, to produce half a dozen—a dozen, five dozen—plays for the sake of my pocket, my material future. Of how little money the novel makes for me I needn't discourse here. The theatre has sought me out—in the person of the good, the yet unseen, Compton. I have listened and considered and reflected, and the matter is transposed to a minor key. To accept the circumstances, in their extreme humility, and do the best I can *in* them: this is the moral of my present situation.

Almost a year elapsed before James could write his play version of *The American.* During that time however he poured into *The Tragic Muse* his feelings about the stage—his contempt for its practical conditions, his delight in the dramatic form. When Gabriel Nash, in a long outburst, describes the problems of writing for the Victorian theatre— and it applies to the contemporary as well—he is speaking for Henry James:

. . . the *omnium gatherum* of the population of a big commercial city at the hour of the day when their taste is at its lowest, flocking out of hideous hotels and restaurants, gorged with food, stultified with buying and selling and with all the other sordid preoccupations of the age, squeezed together in a sweltering mass, disappointed in their seats, timing the author, timing the actor, wishing to get their money back on the spot—all before eleven o'clock. Fancy putting the exquisite before such a tribunal as that! There's not even a question of it. The dramatist wouldn't if he could, and in nine cases out of ten he couldn't if he would. He has to make the basest concessions. One of his principal canons is that he must enable his spectators to catch the suburban trains, which stop at 11:30. What would you think of any other artist—the painter or the novelist—whose governing forces should be the dinner and the suburban trains? The old dramatists didn't defer to them—not so much at least—and that's why they're less and less actable. If they're touched— the large loose men—it's only to be mutilated and trivialised. Besides, they had a simpler civilisation to represent—societies in which the life of man was in action, in passion, in immediate and violent expression. Those things could be put upon the playhouse boards with comparatively little sacrifice of their completeness and their truth. To-day we're so infinitely more reflective and complicated and diffuse that it makes all the difference. What can you do with a character, with an idea, with a feeling, between dinner and the suburban trains? You can give a gross rough sketch of them, but how little you touch them, how bald you leave them! What crudity compared with what the novelist does!

A would-be dramatist approaching his art with so acute a sense of its short-comings and material difficulties was hardly in a frame of mind to attack it bravely. This passage suggests that James already had climbed into the dramatic "straitjacket" of which he was to complain during the coming years. He set about his play-writing with characteristic energy; yet his letters during these early months of what was to prove to be a five-year siege of the theatre betray hesitations, uncertainties, misgivings —a continuation of the inner debate revealed earlier in his journal entries and his novels. He strikes the same notes in all his letters: he is venturing into the theatre for "exclusively mercenary" reasons; he wants his play-writing to be kept a secret until the play is produced; the dramatic form is admirable, the conditions of the British theatre are vulgar and odious. He is secretive to the point of coyness; he sends his script to his sister Alice and solemnly enjoins her not to write to William about it, or at any rate to "give a sign that he must bury what you tell him in tenfold mystery." To which he adds, half-seriously, "but I doubt if even this would be secure—it would be in the *Transcript* the next week." To William he writes that "for all sorts of reasons I desire to be extremely secret, silent and mysterious" about the theatrical enterprises. He explains that this was to be an attempt of the "most resolute and scientific character." He writes: "It is ridiculous at my age, to make only *one* bid for theatrical profit ('one murder makes a villain— millions a hero':) therefore I mean to make—as soon as *may* be—eight or ten."

As Henry continued to be mysterious and secretive about the details of his dramatic work, William in characteristic fashion teased him, saying he assumed the "mysterious fortune-making plans" were probably the "formation of an international 'trust' to produce the plays simultaneously in all the capitals of the earth, or something of the kind." He added: "You ought to know enough critically about the qualities that the stage requires, if you can only coldbloodedly throw in enough action to please the people." Later, when William knew the details, Henry was still cautioning him "please breathe no word of these confidences, as publicity blows on such matters in an injurious and deflowering way. And interests too great to be hurt are at stake."

His need for secrecy was explained by him in a

letter to his brother many months later, after the
failure of one of his projects: "What is heart-break-
ing is the having to *tell* them and talk about them
and answer people's questions (I don't say this for
*you!*) mostly indiscreet and idle. *That,* only, is the
real giving one's self away. There is *no* answer to
be given, or information to be supplied, in relation
to any situation one is in with a theatre or manager. *Silence,* till production takes place, if it is
ever to, is the only thing that meets the dangers and
covers the abysses. Please *know* nothing if anyone
asks you about my affairs. I say nothing myself
whatever. I only do my business and go my way."

Outside his family, Robert Louis Stevenson was
one of a few friends who received James's theatrical
confidences, and yet always in general terms. To
Stevenson he was invariably apologetic: "Don't be
hard on me, simplifying and chastening necessity
has laid its brutal hand on me and I have had to try
and make somehow or other the money I don't
make by literature." In the same letter he refers to
*The American* as his "tribute to the vulgarest of
the muses" and speaks of a "base theatrical errand"
—meaning a rehearsal he is about to attend. He
writes to Stevenson: "My zeal in the affair is only
matched by my indifference," yet in the same letter
he says, "I find the *form* opens out before me as if
it were a kingdom to conquer." And then, as if he
had spoken too kind a word for the theatre, he
promptly adds "a kingdom forsooth of ignorant
brutes of managers and dense cabotins of actors."
Immediately after this there is again an expression
of delight: "All the same, I feel as if I had at last
*found* my form—my real one—that for which pale
fiction is an ineffectual substitute." Again, lest Stevenson take this for genuine enthusiasm, he once
more qualifies: "God grant this unholy truth may
not abide with me more than two or three years—

time to dig out eight or ten rounded masterpieces and make withal enough money to enable me to retire in peace and plenty for the unmolested business of a *little* supreme writing, as distinct from gouging—which is the Form above-mentioned."

To William he had written without qualification a few days earlier: "I feel at last as if I had found my *real* form, which I am capable of carrying far, and for which the pale little art of fiction, as I have practised it, has been, for me, but a limited and restricted substitute. The strange thing is that I always, universally, knew *this* was my more characteristic form—but was kept away from it by a half-modest, half-exaggerated sense of the difficulty (that is, I mean the practical odiousness) of the conditions. But now that I have accepted them and met them, I see that one isn't at all, needfully, their victim, but is, from the moment one *is* anything, one's self, worth speaking of, their *master;* and may use them, command them, squeeze them, lift them up and better them. As for the form *itself,* its honor and inspiration are (*à défaut d'autres*) in its difficulty. If it were easy to write a good play I couldn't and wouldn't think of it; but it is in fact damnably hard (to this truth the paucity of the article—in the English-speaking world—testifies,) and that constitutes a solid respectability—guarantees one's *intellectual* self-respect."

These passages from letters written during the period of the production of *The American* illustrate strikingly Henry James's need to justify his venture into the theatre as if it were some abnormal undertaking, requiring explanation and apology. Allowing for his habitual tone of banter in his correspondence with Stevenson and his addiction to euphemism, it is clear, nevertheless, that the reiterated apologies for the theatre sprang from needs other than to amuse and entertain his friend.

The tone of the letters might be light, carefree, contradictory; the inner content was serious, and derived from a deeply-grounded need to put up a good "front" dramatically speaking. He had made a decision; he was not at all sure of himself; he felt he was straying from the dignified path of a man of letters and he wanted to be certain his friends would not think the less of him for it. The late Victorian theatre was an impoverished institution, lacking the artistic richness and freedom of fiction. Henry James recognized the challenge to improve it. But he was afraid. The best justification he could find was his need to earn money. It was true that the dwindling sales of his books created a greater sense of financial need than had existed earlier. His royalties were, as he complained, pitifully small: but he earned substantial sums from serialization. The *Atlantic* paid him $15 a page for *The Tragic Muse* (a yield of $300 a month) and income from other sources continued to give him a safe margin of security. There was, however, another reason now for his emphasis on pecuniary returns. He had reached his "middle years" beset by feelings of literary inadequacy (in the marketplace) and the thought of the years to come, with the prospect of diminishing returns, deeply disturbed him. Therefore one of his reasons was the desire to "provide for one's old age."

His emphasis on money must be seen in the light of a new friendship, formed at the outset of the dramatic years, with a young American, Wolcott Balestier, a friend of Howells, who arrived in London shortly before the dramatization of *The American* to represent a New York publisher. Lively, energetic, himself a writer of short stories and novels (he later collaborated with Kipling in *The Naulahka*), young Balestier undertook to guide James in his financial arrangements for the plays. With a whole-hearted admiration for the middle-aged novelist, and a characteristic enthusiasm that endeared him to London's literary world, Balestier fired James's imagination with stories of fortunes to be derived from dramatic production. "Dear Suzerain of the Drama," he addressed his letters to James with a flamboyance and flattery that delighted the novelist; and presently James was building great castles in the air based on hypothetical royalties he would derive from his plays in England plus those which would pour in from the American rights and even, he amusedly suggested, from the Australian! The thought of fabulous fortunes, coupled with an awareness of the large incomes of playwrights such as Arthur Pinero, Henry Arthur Jones and Oscar Wilde, made Henry James acutely aware of the smallness of his literary income; and it was small indeed, judged by a dramatist's earnings during the successful run of a play.

## IV. A MOST UNHOLY TRADE

HE THREW himself into his play-writing as one possessed. In all the fifty years of his authorship he was never to create at a pitch of greater or more feverish intensity. He wrote as if he were a soldier engaged in battle and his life depended on the outcome. The words "siege" and "war" recur constantly in his letters. He imaged the world of the theatre as a battleground. He pictured the stage as an "abyss" and by implication placed himself on its brink. He rewrote, he elaborated parts to suit actors and actresses; he contrived happy endings he would never have dreamed of in his novels; he caricatured his fellow countrymen to win laughter from English audiences; he struggled with the "barbarous, the ignorant, the sickening race of managers"; he bowed before "the foul fiend Excision"—speaking of his plays as bloodied, amputated, butchered children. ("Oh, the mutilated, brutally simplified, massacred little play!") Behind the half-exaggerated and elaborate irony and mockery of his pronouncements lay a deep and serious purpose, that of meeting the stage on its terms. "Forget not," he exploded one day to his publisher, William Heinemann, "that you write for the stupid—that is, that your maximum of refinement must meet the minimum of intelligence of the audience—the intelligence, in other words, of the biggest ass it may conceivably contain." And he added: "It is a most unholy trade!"

Scenario succeeded scenario—we shall never know exactly how many—and were circulated among the London managers. At rehearsals of *The American* James mounted the stage to demonstrate to the actors how parts should be played, drawing upon his memory of bits of "business" seen on the stage of the Théâtre Français: "I spent upwards of five hours yesterday on the deadly cold stage of the Portsmouth Theatre (the 'ladies' had *such* red noses!) going at them tooth and nail, without pause, and then two more with my *grand premier rôle* at his lodgings, coaching him with truly psychological intensity; acting, intonating everything *for* him and showing him simply *how!* The authorship (in any sense worthy of the name) of a play only *begins* when it is written, and I see that one's creation of it doesn't terminate till one has gone with it every inch of the way to the rise of the curtain on the first night." During his five dramatic years, however, he had only two productions upon which to lavish such effort; the majority of his plays remained unproduced.

He was in a state of constant tension: accustomed to the freedom of fiction he found himself in a theatre wedged between the backdrop and the proscenium, reaching beyond the footlights to an audience that asked to be entertained and pleased "on the spot." At first he relished the flare of the gaslight, the painted faces, the rituals and superstitions of the stage, the high hopes, the realities backstage and the make-believe on-stage. The reactions of the audience stirred and excited him; the modest, unobtrusive "observer" that was Henry James enjoyed hearing his work applauded, and humanly delighted in the call of "Author, author" that brought him before the people he had sought to entertain during the provincial run of *The American* in 1890. He felt the challenge of the dramatic art, and was stimulated by his contact with creatures of flesh and blood, he who had lived in the fantasied world of his novelist's study. Yet disillusion set in rapidly; inner nightmares plagued him; his anxieties overflowed to disturb and confuse his relations with actors and managers. At fifty, and a famous man of letters, he was impatient over the characteristic delays of the theatre: "The great stumbling block in the whole business is the question of Time—the slowness, the waiting, the delays which are a large part of the very essence of managerial production. They talk of years as we talk of months and I am handicapped by having begun too late and being too old: I ought to have come to it ten years ago. But I shall vanquish all the same."

Recognizing this, he was, nevertheless, unprepared for the theatrical rebuffs which are the common lot of actor and playwright. The children of his brain, upon which he lavished so much ingenuity during the long mornings in De Vere Gardens, lingered ignored in the managerial offices. James was artist enough—and human enough—to feel deep anguish at such treatment. He pleaded, he argued, he worked, he revised, he compromised, and in the end, with the jeers of an audience ringing in his ears, he fled back to his study, to the sanctuary and great good place that had been waiting for him all the time of his struggle in the outer world, exclaiming, as he had many times before:

"I may have been meant for the Drama—God Knows!—but I certainly wasn't meant for the Theatre."

### 1.

We can plot the chart of Henry James's dramatic fever from the casual allusions, hints, veiled vague references to his theatrical enterprises in his letters —information grudgingly vouchsafed to an inquiring older brother, or on occasions to intimate friends close to his efforts in London. *The American,* written early in 1890, was an open secret since it went into production that autumn (and ran for seventy nights in London); but other plays are identified often by numbers in his letters and we are never certain in what order they were written since he only named three of them. Between November and December 1890 he wrote *Tenants,* first known as *Mrs. Vibert,* for John Hare; in mid-December he began "Play #3" intended for Compton, who had produced *The American,* and this was completed by January 10, 1891. It was either *The Reprobate* or *The Album*—the two works he described later as designed to be played in country towns and which he ultimately admitted to Edmund Gosse he had intended for the Compton Comedy Company. On February 6, 1891, he wrote to William that he was attacking "my fourth" but we have no way of knowing what this play was and whether he completed it. In the autumn of 1891 he discussed a play for Augustin Daly, the American manager who was planning a London season, and in December of that year he was writing a "three-act

contemporary comedy" again, for Edward Compton
—this again either *Reprobate* or *Album*.

He had completed the play for Daly by the summer of 1892 for he read *Mrs. Jasper,* later re-titled
*Disengaged,* to Ada Rehan during August of that
year, and in November he was planning a second
play for her which, however, ultimately became
the one-act play he wrote for Ellen Terry. In May
of 1893 he sketched the scenario for a "three-act
comedy pure and simple" which later that year he
offered to George Alexander, the matinee idol and
enterprising manager of the St. James's. He spoke
at this time also of a play tentatively titled *Monte
Carlo.* In May or June of 1893 he set down his first
note for the dramatization of *The Chaperon* following a suggestion made to him by Arthur Pinero that
his short story of that name had in it all the ingre-
dients of a high comedy.

That summer, at Ramsgate, he wrote *Guy Domville* for Alexander. In November 1893, while nego-
tiating with Daly for the production of *Disengaged,*
which he revised, and with Alexander for the production of *Domville,* he had "almost finished . . .
another three act play" for Comyns Carr, the London art critic who had leased the Comedy Theatre.
Carr was waiting to decide after seeing the third
act. From an allusion to the *Monte Carlo* play in
his notebooks at this time we may speculate that this
work may have been intended for Carr. By this
time Henry James's desk was clearly piled high
with scenarios and half-written plays. On December
7, 1893, he slips into a letter to Elizabeth Robins a
final exclamatory sentence: "I have begun another
play!" and three weeks later, before his Christmas
fire, he is dreaming up still another play for Compton, tentatively named *The Promise.* In 1894 he
sets down the scenario for this play, and lays it
aside when Compton shows no interest in it. (Two

years later he turned it into the novel, *The Other House,* and a dozen years after that he turned the novel into a play.) During this year he made the first note of the theme that was to flower into *The Wings of the Dove,* conceiving it first also as a play.

How many of these numerous projects were completed? how many absorbed into his fiction? how many scrapped? We know little more today than James's correspondents did when they received his chary confidences. The two plays which saw production during the 1890's were never published. Four comedies written during this period which never reached the stage were issued in book form (the two series of *Theatricals*); a one-act play was converted into a short story; a scenario was converted into a novel; and much later a three-act comedy into a novel. It is quite likely that the novelist did not scrap any of his completed plays, since we know that he did not like work to go to waste. Certain of the "plays" written during these crowded months existed only as extended scenarios and these he seems to have destroyed. Perhaps some day some portions of plays and scenarios may turn up among the papers of the late Victorian actor-managers. Yet even here there is not much likelihood, since James usually reclaimed his scripts. We may surmise that he made copious notes for his plays in those notebooks which he destroyed; the few pages of the first note for *The Chaperon* which survive (because he had hopes of writing this play) were torn from a scribbler such as he used for his notebooks and break off in the middle of a tantalizing sentence. A few words more and we might have learned something about *Monte Carlo.* Searches instituted some years ago by the editor of this volume among the papers of Sir John Hare and J. Comyns Carr yielded neither scenarios nor letters.

2.

The four comedies which Henry James published
as a "melancholy subterfuge," seeking to console
himself with "the performance imaginary," are con-
ventional and contrived in the tradition of French
comedy of manners. James resorts freely to melodrama to untangle his plots, he is prodigal, after
the manner of the time, in his use of asides and
employs the catch-phrase unhesitatingly as a humorous resource. His characters belong to the stock
company of theatrical tradition—"strong" women,
double dealers, doting mothers, flirts and philan-
derers, deep-dyed villains and virtuous, bumbling
protagonists. An adventuress seeks to "place" her
illegitimate son in the social hierarchy; there is an
intrigue to deprive a rightful heir of his fortune;
a practical joke results in a man's engagement to a
woman, in spite of himself, and there is an intrigue
to "disengage" him; a young man, considered a
reprobate, develops into a self-asserting individual.
There are echoes of Dumas *fils* and Augier in these
plays; there is the *coup de théâtre* in the manner
of Sardou; the *ficelle* is strained to the breaking
point.

Henry James was seeking to write crisp, witty,
epigrammatic comedy at the same time as Oscar
Wilde, and these comedies inevitably invite comparison with those of his contemporary. James's
plays have more substance, weightier machinery,
much plot, considerable drollery, less wit, but much
sharper caricature. Wilde's plays are tinsel and
pasteboard; his people are mouthpieces for his
cleverness. There is less gloss in James's comedies,
but at every turn one is conscious of the hand of
an experienced artist engaged in characterizing
people and setting them within the scenic frame.

The fundamental difference between Henry James
and Oscar Wilde (James called him the "unspeak-
able one") so far as the failure of one and the success of the other in the theatre is concerned, resides
in their approach to the public. Wilde remained
true to the figure of himself he had long before
projected—that of a cool, arrogant coiner of witty
phrases and epigrams, utterly indifferent to his
public but aware of how to please it. James described to a friend the first night of *Lady Winder-
mere's Fan* in 1892: Oscar "with a metallic blue
carnation in his buttonhole and a cigarette in his
fingers" made a curtain speech. "The speech, which,
alas, was stupid, was only to say that he judged the
audience felt the play to be merely as charming as
he did." The audience accepted his condescension
and laughed at it. James could not be indifferent
to his public. He was trying too hard to please. The
public, or the managers who read his plays, sensed
this strain, and could neither laugh at him, as at
Wilde, nor sympathize with him.

This feeling of anxiety in James is reflected in
the prefaces to the two volumes of *Theatricals*.
Beneath the polished surface of their prose one can
sense the heartbreak. Stripped of their urbane ex-
teriors the prefaces express a kind of helplessness
in the face of conditions with which the novelist
could not cope. In arraying the dramatist's difficulties James also expressed the apprehension he
felt—fear of being supersubtle, fear, coupled with
a very natural resentment, of the mutilation of his
plays by managers, fear of the limitations imposed
upon him by the clock. It is no wonder that the
shrewd reviewer of the *Daily Chronicle,* discussing
*Theatricals,* saw in James's "exaggerated respect and
exaggerated contempt" for the stage an ambivalence
that foredoomed his theatrical undertakings.

"He is fascinated by the very difficulty," wrote

the perspicacious reviewer, "yet in his heart he despises himself for yielding to the fascination." The theatrical tight rope, the abyss, the straitjacket, existed in James's own mind. If Henry James could have approached the theatre with genuine confidence, in the manner in which he wrote his fiction, we should probably be telling a different story today.

### 3.

He had thought of himself as a double-personality, a monk writing in his cell, a man of the world moving about in society, observing, noting, recording. Now this fantasy reasserted itself. Henry James, the dramatist, walked abroad in the London daylight, was strong, vigorous, masculine, a soldier laying siege to the citadel of the theatre, a champion of Ibsen, a gallant defender of the dramatic art. The other Henry James, the literary man, sat in his Kensington study, contriving scenarios and plays, cursing managers but continuing to write —always writing. He wrote a story about such a double-personality in "The Private Life," during the second of his dramatic years, attaching it to the figure of Robert Browning, whom he envisaged as possessing an *alter ego,* a writer who created his poetry in private while an unpoetic, a more prosaic, "other self" moved through the London drawing-rooms. Henry James worried at the "dramatic, the unspeakably theatric form," but he dipped his pen also into the "other ink—the sacred fluid of fiction." Nothing was more soothing, he noted in 1893, than "to remember that literature sits patient at my door, and that I have only to lift the latch to let in the exquisite little form that is, after all, nearest my heart." (Thus far had he come since his outburst to William James two years earlier about the "pale little art of fiction" and his enthusiastic assertion that the drama was "my more character-istic form.")

For he continued to practice the fictional form and "pale" is the last word most critics would apply to the stories written during the dramatic years. He had forsworn the novel; he confined himself only to the short story (*à la Maupassant,* he told himself) and with an ardor all the more intense, since his story-writing provided an escape from the frustrations of the theatre. Between the production of *The American* in 1890 and *Guy Domville* in the first days of 1895, he wrote nineteen tales, including such masterpieces as "The Real Thing," "The Altar of the Dead," "Sir Edmund Orme," "The Chaperon," "The Marriages," "The Death of the Lion," "The Coxen Fund," and thirteen articles ranging from memorials to his lately dead friends, James Russell Lowell, Fanny Kemble, and Robert Browning, to critical discussions of Ibsen and Flau-bert. He saw six volumes of tales and essays through the press during the dramatic years; his output continued to be large, but his determination to write no more long novels for serialization reduced his literary earnings considerably. Writing unpro-duced plays was proving a costly process.

Into the tales written during these troubled years there flowed very little of his actual theatrical ex-perience. Only one of the nineteen stories dealt di-rectly with a theatrical subject; this was "Nona Vincent," written immediately after the production of *The American* and reflecting in every detail James's adventures on the road and in London with the Compton Comedy Company. Allan Way-worth, the young, fastidious, nervous playwright, clinging to the safely-married and all-wise Mrs. Alsager, was the Henry James who had read his plays to his friends Mrs. John L. Gardner and Mrs. Hugh Bell. Henry James's boast to his brother: "I

feel at last as if I had found my *real* form" was
Wayworth's "mastery of the scenic idea"; Henry
James's view that the theatre was an "abyss of
vulgarity and platitude" was Wayworth's "managerial abyss." Henry James's remark in the preface
to the second series of *Theatricals* that a playwright
must seek economy by the "periodical throwing
overboard of the cargo to save the ship" anticipates
Wayworth's "You were perpetually throwing over
the cargo to save the ship."

If the overt material did not go into his other
stories, the emotions arising from his play-writing
did. A reader examining the stories, unaware of
James's activities during these years, would discover in them evidence of a prevailing anxiety and
an ever-deepening sense of frustration. He had
written only four ghostly tales between his twenty-
second and forty-seventh years; now the super-
natural element appears in a series of tales—the
daylight ghost of "Sir Edmund Orme," the overwhelming night-time spirit of the Family in "Owen
Wingrave," the supernatural-fantastic of "The Private Life," the operation of clairvoyance or tele-
pathy and benign supernaturalism of "Sir Domi-
nick Ferrand" and "Nona Vincent" reflected James's
uneasiness. He wrote twelve such tales during the
'nineties, including the celebrated "Turn of the
Screw," his ultimate record of nightmare set down
in the aftermath of dramatic defeat. At the same
time there came from his pen tales of writers unappreciated and ignored, public failures, private
"successes," triumphant only in their art. These are
almost completely autobiographical since Henry
James identified himself with the writers he por-
trayed. The stories were derived (as James cau-
tiously said in a preface a dozen years later) "in
each case, from some noted adventure, some felt
embarrassment, some extreme predicament, of the

artist enamored of perfection." *Some felt embarrassment.* We do not have to seek far to discover the
person who *felt* the embarrassment. He published
a volume after his dramatic years containing four
stories, two dealing with unsuccessful writers, and
called it *Embarrassments.* In 1893, the year of his
fiftieth birthday, James published only one short
story. He called it "The Middle Years." It is the
story of a writer who, in middle life, feels that it
has taken him too long to learn his craft. "His
development had been abnormally slow, almost
grotesquely gradual. He had been hindered and
retarded by experience. . . . It had taken too much
of life to produce too little of his art. At such a
rate a first existence was too short."

"Poor Dencombe," the writer, pleads in vain for
a second existence in which to write the great works
he has in his mind and dies realizing that he has
accomplished all he has been capable of doing. The
dying Dencombe whispers to the admiring young
doctor at his side: "It's frustration that doesn't
count." And the admiring young doctor philosophi-
cally replies: "Frustration's only life."

Frustration was only life. At the end of the year
in which he wrote these words, Henry James angrily withdrew his comedy, *Disengaged,* from Augustin Daly, after a difference with the producer,
gritted his teeth and wrote to William:

". . . à la guerre comme à la guerre. I mean to
wage this war ferociously for one year more—1894
—and then (unless the victory and the spoils have
not by that become more proportionate than
hitherto to the humiliations and vulgarities and
disgusts, all the dishonor and chronic insult in-
curred) to 'chuck' the whole intolerable experiment
and return to the more elevated and more independent courses." And he added: "The whole odiousness of the thing lies in the connection between the

drama and the theatre. The one is admirable in its interest and difficulty, the other loathesome in its conditions."

4.

"One year more—1894." Henry James's notes during this year recurrently brood upon death. Entry after entry betrays his feeling of frustration, his sense of time irretrievably lost, the belief that had grown in the five years since his last novel that he was a figure unwanted in the artistic life of his time. At the beginning of the year he wrote "The idea of *death* both checked and caught me . . ." and it became the *leitmotif* of the successive notebook entries: ideas for stories of men living a kind of death-in-life, of men who have died emotionally or who have bartered passion for material opportunities and live on in a mockery of life. During this year he set down his fantasy of the literary "lion" discovered late in his career and smothered by uncritical adulation, finally dying of it. He also set down the first plan or a story of "some young creature . . . who, at 20, on the threshold of a life that has seemed boundless, is suddenly condemned to death." Eight years later this became *The Wings of the Dove*. During this year he also wrote his lament for the neglected dead which grew in his hands into "The Altar of the Dead"—the story of the great blazing altar on which George Stransom set his candles, symbols of the tomb, in the knowledge that a candle one day would be lit for him. During 1894 James published only three tales and two of them have Death in their titles— "The Death of the Lion" and "The Altar of the Dead." To the volume in which he assembled these stories, together with "The Coxen Fund," written during a sad summer in Italy that year, a story of death-in-life, of a writer who fritters away his talent in talk, and "The Middle Years," the story of the author seeking a second chance, he gave the lugubrious title of *Terminations*.

1894 was a year of terminations and Henry James knew it. *One year more*. *Guy Domville* was to be the final test and all his hopes and dreams of the past five years went into that play. Rehearsals began during December of 1894, and for a few days Henry James re-experienced all the high elation—and sharp conflict—of the dramatist he had painted in "Nona Vincent." The year of gloom came to a gloomy end with word of the death of his old friend Robert Louis Stevenson in Samoa; and the new year was but five days old when Henry James walked out on the stage of the St. James's Theatre to face the ultimate rejection from the public he had tried to please. The terminal episode of his five dramatic years lasted but a few seconds.

## V. THE LAST OF THE DOMVILLES

### 1.

*Guy Domville* was written by Henry James during the summer of 1893 at Ramsgate on the Channel for George Alexander, the popular and highly successful young manager of the St. James's Theatre. Alexander's production of *The Second Mrs. Tanqueray* had convinced James that he had at last found a manager for whom he could write a serious play. He actually discussed three play projects with him and promised scenarios of all of them: the first was a romantic costume play about a young man destined for the priesthood; the second was "a three-act comedy, pure and simple," and the third "a three-act contemporary play, less purely a comedy, but on a subject very beautiful to my sense." The first subject appealed to James, however, and instead of submitting his three "exhibits" he sent

Alexander the completed first act of the play about the priestly candidate and a scenario of the remaining two acts. Alexander liked it. They began to discuss terms almost immediately.

The idea for *Guy Domville* had been noted by James a year earlier at Lausanne. He had just spent some days in Venice, after a journey through Italy with Paul Bourget and his wife, and he wrote in his notebook:

> Situation of that once-upon-a-time member of an old Venetian family (I forget which), who had become a monk, and who was taken almost forcibly out of his convent and brought back into the world in order to keep the family from becoming extinct. He was the last *rejeton*—it was absolutely *necessary* for him to marry. Adapt this somehow or other to today.

Immediately below this note, in one of the lists of names James regularly entered in his notebook for use in his novels and plays, occurs the name Domville. The subject of the play touched the novelist's life closely; it dealt with the conflict of many of his heroes—the question of participation and action in life or withdrawal from it. *Guy Domville* was a reiteration of the problems presented in *The Tragic Muse,* and it foreshadowed another tale James was to write some years later, "The Great Good Place," whose hero, George Dane, a writer (with initials similar to Guy Domville's) is translated in a dream from worldly pressures to a monastery-like retreat, "some great abode of an Order, some mild Monte Cassino, some Grande Chartreuse." The name Dane figures in the same list as Domville, and we may speculate that in James's mind it may have been associated with Dane Hall at Harvard where James himself had made an important decision renouncing the study of law for the practice of letters—which he discusses in an as yet unpublished autobiographical fragment speculating upon "the turning point of my life."

On another level *Guy Domville* was a projection of James's actual conflict in the theatre—that is the "world" represented by London "show business" of the time and the alternative, ever possible for James, of retreat to his literary study. Many other elements enter into the creation of this play: the novelist's deep interest in Catholicism as a "refuge" and a retreat, his own sense of "dedication" to his art expressed in several of his tales of the literary life, notably in "The Lesson of the Master," in which James half-humorously, half-seriously advocated celibacy for the artist; his fantasy of the artist as a double-personality, moving in the world, on the one hand, but living, on the other hand, a separate anchorite life in the privacy of his study ("Benvolio," "The Private Life"), his deep sense that the fraternity of letters constituted an "Order" of the pledged and dedicated, analogous to the priesthood. Students of "sources" might find also a congruity between *Guy Domville* and the fact that the one novel of his friend Howells which James reviewed twice in one month was *A Foregone Conclusion*—the story of a Venetian priest who falls in love with an American girl and is unable to resolve his conflict between the spirit and the flesh.

The partnership of Henry James and George Alexander represented the linking of a dedicated man of letters with a dapper matinee idol. Henry Irving had once remarked to Alexander at a rehearsal, "Now Alexander, not quite so much Piccadilly." The actor-manager *was* "Piccadilly" to his fingertips—a dandy of the 1890's endowed by nature with straight, handsome features and an excellent pair of legs that made him partial to costume pieces. When he was not displaying his legs in breeches of another era or in riding boots, he wore the most perfectly creased trousers in the West End. In an era when trousers were worn baggy, Alexander's were pressed to perfection. They were the talk of the clubs and the subject of cartoons in *Punch*. Alexander's trousers were a distinct part of a man variously described as a tailor's dummy and hard-headed businessman; but for his acting the critics had chary praise. "Mr. Alexander," wrote Bernard Shaw of one of his performances, "gave us a finished impersonation of Mr. George Alexander." Nevertheless he had his loyal following, and many a lady sighed away an afternoon over his handsome and romantic characterizations.

His contemporaries agreed that Alexander was not a man of large imagination; and he compensated for this by a kind of furious efficiency. His theatre was a model of management. If he lacked the depth that makes for greatness on the stage, if he was what critics tend to describe, when they feel charitable, as "competent," he was nevertheless pleasant, affable, shrewd. He had taken the measure of his talents and knew how to make the most of them. He was careful to surround himself with good actors, but careful, too, that he should not be eclipsed. In one notable instance he was, and his quarrels with Mrs. Patrick Campbell, on stage and off—the meeting of a tempestuous and passionate actress with a cool and calculating man of attitudes —are a part of the theatrical history of the 1890's. Alexander's loyal "fans" would fill his house for a month even if his play were pronounced a failure. And he showed, on the whole, considerable discrimination in his choice of plays—so long as they had good strutting parts for him.

Alexander's terms, as might be expected in the case of such a hard-headed practical individual, were stiff. He offered James £5 a night, but placed a ceiling of £2,000 on royalties with full rights in the play to go to him after the ceiling was attained. "I should be obliged to you if you can put the case to me more dazzlingly another way," the author wrote to the matinee idol. We do not know how "dazzlingly" Alexander finally put it. James brought the completed play to him during the autumn of 1893 in the hope of an early production after the run of *Mrs. Tanqueray.* To his chagrin he now discovered that Alexander was committed to do a play by Henry Arthur Jones ahead of his own. This meant a long wait. James had, at this time, a difference with Augustin Daly over his comedy *Disengaged,* and this accumulation of discouragements and delays caused him to write, as we have seen, that he would wage the theatrical struggle for "one year more."

It took exactly another year. Alexander finally began rehearsing the play in December 1894. A few weeks before, the author and the actor-manager went over the script. Alexander asked for the elimination of certain parts and certain changes in his role. This was, Henry wrote to his brother, the "hideous, supreme ordeal." Later he exclaimed of *Guy Domville,* "Oh, the mutilated, brutally simplified, massacred little play!" In October 1894 a few acting copies of the play were printed "in intense secrecy, for use in the theatre." Jones's *The Masqueraders* ended its run in November, and Alexander went to bed with an attack of German measles, while the novelist fretted through the two more weeks of unexpected delay. The first reading of the play to the assembled cast took place on Friday, December 7, 1894, and Henry James, who had looked forward to this moment, was forced by a sore throat to abdicate in favor of Alexander, and sit by silently while the actor-manager discussed the piece, scene by scene and act by act.

His letters of the next month tell the story of the rehearsals and of his mounting agitation, as, day after day and, toward the end, twice a day, he went to the St. James's, sat alone in the dim theatre, watching his work assume shape and proffering criticisms and suggestions. The cast was good. Henry wrote to his brother that the play would be "exquisitely mounted, dressed &c and as well acted as London can act. My only anxiety is as to how Alexander will carry the weight of his own part—which is a very beautiful and interesting one. So awfully much depends on him."

The play had originally been titled *The Hero,* then tentatively *Guy Domville,* and finally this title was kept although Henry wrote to William, "I hate it." He made the concession to Alexander, however, since "the said Guy Domville is himself." James went on to ask his brother to "unite in family prayer for me on Saturday, January 5 at 8.30 . . . spare a thought to the lone and nervous dramatic artist." On New Year's Day 1895 he wrote to Mrs. Bell that "the dew of agony is already on my brow." He began to debate whether he should attend his first night. In talk with Edmund Gosse it was suggested that James should remain in a near-by pub and beguile the "tremulous" hours between 8:30 and 11. On January 3, the novelist announced, "I have changed my policy. I recognize that the only way for me to arrive at 10 o'clock with any patience is to *do* something active or at least positive; so I have had the luminous idea of going to see some other play." He added: "I am more or less, already under chloroform."

2.

The first in the series of unusual incidents that accompanied the opening night of *Guy Domville* occurred on the afternoon of the climactic day at the Sloane Street post office in Chelsea. Two ladies, whose identity was never established, created a flurry among the postal employes by dispatching an unsigned telegram to George Alexander: "With hearty wishes for a complete failure." Alexander received the message but he was merciful. He did not show it to his nervous author until after the performance.

Henry James had seldom been in such a state of agitation. As on the occasion of *The American,* in the late afternoon, he tried to walk away from his nerves. Finally he returned to his De Vere Gardens flat and dashed off a series of letters to friends and relatives. "One can have a big danger, in the blessed theatre, even with a small thing," he wrote to his friend, Edward Warren, the architect. To William James he mailed one of the *Guy Domville* playbills and wrote to him: "I am counting on some Psychical intervention from you—this is really the time to show your stuff. . . . The omens, Thank God, are decently good. But what are omens? *Domine in manus tuas—!* This is a time when a man wants a religion . . . my hand shakes and I can only write that I am your plucky, but, all the same, lonely and terrified Henry." The letter is, indeed, in a pathetically shaky and almost illegible hand.

James had selected the theatre and the play with which to fill the evening while his own play would be running its course. He would go to the Haymarket to see Oscar Wilde's *An Ideal Husband.* It was an easy walk to Alexander's theatre. He had never been one of Oscar Wilde's admirers, but he had followed his career with a kind of fascinated amazement. Wilde, at the time of *Guy Domville,* was at the height of his fame—and within a few weeks of his tragic trial. At the Haymarket, James found himself sitting in his stall amid a fashionable audience. He listened attentively to the "Oscarisms" and was increasingly unnerved by the audience's delighted laughter. The epigrams burst like well-timed firecrackers. "Men can be analyzed, women merely adored." "Only dull people are brilliant at breakfast." "Morality is simply the attitude we adopt toward people whom we personally dislike." Henry James's agitation grew rather than diminished. The play did not have the soothing effect he had anticipated. He felt uneasy, afraid, lonely. His anxiety gave way to alarm.

### 3.

While the author of *Guy Domville* sat uneasily in his stall at the Haymarket, carriage after carriage deposited ladies in rich wraps and shimmering gowns and well-groomed, fashionably dressed gentlemen before the St. James's Theatre. The combination of a George Alexander first night and the first original play by an American writer who had chosen to make his home in England, had proved irresistible to the London social world. It was an audience of celebrities, one of the most distinguished ever assembled in a London theatre.

There was one group, however, which laid no claim to distinction. It had queued up for some hours in the raw, biting cold at the entrances to the pit and gallery, shivering and stamping its feet as it waited for the doors to open. It was doubtful whether many of these theatregoers had ever heard of Henry James. They came in search of an evening's entertainment. They knew they could rely on "Alick." Any play with "Alick" in it was worth seeing.

Inside, the theatre was bright and cheerful. Alexander took pride in an up-to-date house ("the theatre is lighted by electricity," the playbills proudly announced). There was a rustle of silks as the elaborately attired ladies, in glistening jewelry, took their places, and a hither-and-thithering in the aisles and between the boxes. Necks were craned to see the celebrities—there seem to have been only celebrities in the stalls that night.

Looking at this brilliant house, in the bright light of its new electric bulbs, we see the great artists of London there, Sir Edward Burne-Jones, bearded and sedate; the academician Sir Frederick Leighton, whose suave personality Henry James had embodied in a short story three years earlier; George Frederick Watts, creator of elaborate and much-admired canvases; George du Maurier, one of James's closest friends, nearing the end of his career first as cartoonist for *Punch* and then as the author of *Peter Ibbetson* and *Trilby;* the fashionable illustrators Frank D. Millet and Alfred Parsons. John Singer Sargent has come to see the work of his countryman, accompanied by the slim and handsome W. Graham Robertson, a gifted artist and writer whose portrait Sargent had painted two years earlier and exhibited with much success.

The author's loyal literary lady friends are there in force: Mrs. W. K. Clifford, novelist and playwright; Mrs. Humphry Ward, whose success in the literary market was a Victorian phenomenon; Mrs. Hugh Bell, who had had a play produced at the Théâtre Français. The walrus-mustached, ubiquitous man of letters, Edmund Gosse, is there almost as excited as James himself; and the novelist's compatriot, F. Marion Crawford; the journalist H. D. Traill and Thomas Anstey Guthrie ("F. Anstey"), novelist and a valued contributor to *Punch;* William Lestocq, actor, dramatist, manager; Elizabeth Robins, who has come with Mrs. Bell, are guests in Henry James's box, with Mrs. Charles Lawrence, Lady Airlie, Philip Burne-Jones and Douglas Ainslie; also present are Kate and Florence Terry, Ellen's sisters, who will at the rise of the curtain

be watching another sister, Marion, in the play.
There are other popular actresses in the house as
well: Mrs. Bernard Beere and Fanny Brough, and
Lily Hanbury who is Mrs. Alexander's guest, sitting
with her in the special box that Mrs. Alexander
occupies on all of "Alick's" first nights. It commands a perfect view of the stage—and of her
handsome husband.

4.

Most of the members of that audience could have
pointed out three of London's first-rank dramatic
critics—William Archer of the *World,* A. B. Walkley, then of the *Star* (later of the *Times*) and the
irascible Ibsen-hater, Clement Scott of the *Daily
Telegraph.* Some would have pointed also to a
red-bearded Bernard Shaw, who sat in the stalls in
a modest brown jacket suit while most of his critical
colleagues wore boiled shirts and black or white
ties. He was then better known to the operagoers
at Covent Garden as a vigorous and discriminating
music critic than as a man of the theatre. Shaw's
face was very white and his whiskers very red. He
had already offered substantial proof of his creative
ability, but his major works were yet to be written.
*Widowers' Houses* had been produced by J. T.
Grein at the Independent Theatre and *Arms and
the Man* at the Avenue. That very week Shaw had
ceased to write musical criticism for the *World* and
agreed to do dramatic criticism for Frank Harris
on the *Saturday Review.* He had entered upon his
critical duties four days earlier. *Guy Domville* was
the third play he reviewed.

Few would have pointed to young H. G. Wells.
Mr. Wells, more conformist than Mr. Shaw, came
dressed in a brand-new evening suit, made for him
at twenty-four hours' notice three days before when
he had discovered that he was to be the *Pall Mall*

*Gazette* drama critic. He had reviewed *An Ideal Husband* two nights before; this was his second chore and he was not destined to do many more, for he had already sold *The Time Machine* for £100 and its publication, a few weeks later, was to start him on the long and famous road in English letters which he subsequently travelled. Wells was never much interested in the theatre; it seemed to him artificial and without significance in a world of scientific realities. He was too stubborn a realist to accept the make-believe that goes on behind the footlights and too rigorous a journalist to care for an "art" whose essence is illusion. Years later he said that the incidents of this night at the St. James's only confirmed his distaste for the theatre. He never seriously tried to write a play. "I was forming a conception of a new sort of human community with an unprecedented way of life and it seemed to me to be a minor detail whether this boxed-up performance of plays, would occur at all in that ampler existence I anticipated."

Wells's denial of the fundamental appeal of the scenic art on his utopian grounds (a form of make-believe he *was* willing to indulge in) was not shared, happily, by Shaw. He too wanted new worlds, socialist worlds, but he found he could best preach them within the boxed-up performances that Wells disdained. And great national theatres were included in Bernard Shaw's blueprints for a future world. It was on this night that Wells spoke to Shaw for the first time. They left the theatre together, walking northward to their respective lodgings.

There was still another unknown figure in that audience, almost as obscure as Wells. This was Arnold Bennett, lately come to London and then working for a magazine called *Woman* of which he eventually became editor. Bennett did not sign his name to his theatrical column, which he called "Music and Mummery." The review that he wrote of *Guy Domville* is signed Cécile.

G.B.S., for so Shaw signed his reviews, was thirty-nine. Wells was twenty-nine, Bennett twenty-eight. They sat, unknown to each other, among the greater celebrities of the time, waiting for the play to begin.

The orchestra fussed its way through the "Guy Domville Prelude," a special concoction for the occasion by Walter Slaughter, the orchestra's conductor. There was a curtain raiser, *Too Many by Half* by Julian Field, which gave the latecomers some leeway, and which Shaw described as "deftly turned out from old and seasoned materials," and "capital fun for the audience." The evening at least began on a note of laughter.

## 5.

The curtain rose on one of George Alexander's expensive and elaborately realistic settings which were the pride of his management. The scene was a garden at Porches, the time 1780. Clustering rose bushes and honeysuckle trailed round quaint lattice windows; borders of multi-colored flowers and a closecut privet hedge set a tone of peaceful rural charm. In this setting the dramatist developed with great simplicity his delicate tale of love and renunciation, of a young man called upon to choose between a career in the Church and his obligation to his family to marry and perpetuate his line—a young man who, unaware of his love for the heroine, and of her love for him, pleads with her to lend an attentive ear to the suit of his best friend. The graceful and rhythmic dialogue of the first act delighted the audience. Marion Terry, as Mrs. Peverel, the object of Frank Humber's and Guy Domville's love, was an appealing figure. She wore a

silken gown of pale gray, bordered with tiny frills
and caught in to the waist by black velvet bows.
She also wore a quaint loosely hanging jacket, with
muslin collars and ruched edges; and her Leghorn
hat was tied by narrow black velvet strings. Her
voice, her manner, her warmth, her tone—she
seems to have put a great deal of feeling into the
part—charmed everyone. To Guy, who is the tutor
of her young son, she is a maternal image he does
not even dare to admit to himself he loves. Alexander, in sober black raiment, as befits a young
churchman, provided a contrasting figure on the
brightly lit stage. The actors caught and sustained
the romantic mood. The dialogue fell with a pleas-
ing sound on the music critic's ears of Bernard
Shaw, who described it "as grateful to my ear as the
music of Mozart's *Entführung aus dem Serail* would
be after a year of *Ernani* and *Il Trovatore.*"

---

## ST. JAMES'S THEATRE.

SOLE LESSEE AND MANAGER - - - MR. GEORGE ALEXANDER.

---

### Saturday, Jan. 5th, 1895, & Every Evening at 9,

A Play in Three Acts,

### By HENRY JAMES,

ENTITLED

# "GUY DOMVILLE."

| | | | |
|---|---|---|---|
| Guy Domville | - | - | Mr. GEORGE ALEXANDER |
| Lord Devenish | - | - | Mr. ELLIOT |
| Frank Humber | - | - | Mr. HERBERT WARING |
| George Round | - | (Lieutenant, R.N.) | Mr. H. V. ESMOND |
| Servant | - | - | Mr. FRANK DYALL |
| Mrs. Peverel | - | - | Miss MARION TERRY |
| Mrs. Domville | - | - | Mrs. EDWARD SAKER |
| Mary Brasier | - | - | Miss EVELYN MILLARD |
| Fanny | - | - | Miss IRENE VANBRUGH |
| Milliners | - | { | Miss BLANCHE WILMOT<br>Miss VIOLET LYSTER |

PERIOD - - 1780.

| | | | |
|---|---|---|---|
| Act I. | - | - | THE GARDEN AT PORCHES |
| Act II. | - | MRS. DOMVILLE'S RESIDENCE AT RICHMOND |
| Act III. | - | - | AN INTERIOR AT PORCHES |

Temptation arrived in the form of Lord Devenish, a designing, evil, Mephistophelean figure played by W. G. Elliot with operatic broadness. A. B. Walkley spoke of his acting as "a prolonged grimace, a caricature, too uniformly in the violent style of Hogarth," while Shaw accused him of "withering all sense and music of Mr. James's lines with a diction which I forbear to describe." The *St. James Gazette* suggested that the part might be rendered a "little less glaringly obnoxious" and *Today* said flatly: "Willie Elliot was hopelessly at sea as a wicked nobleman and looked as if he belonged to a comic ballet and had strayed into the St. James's by mistake." (In his memoirs, years later, Elliot recalled that during rehearsals James had asked him to try to make Lord Devenish appear "as much of a gentleman as is feasible—possible—to you.")

The curtain fell, the lights came on, and a deeply stirred audience rose for the first intermission. The critics agreed that Henry James had written a beautiful first act. They referred later to its "tender idyllic grace" and the "unforced truthfulness of the dialogue." William Archer found it a "masterly and exquisite piece of emotional comedy"; Arnold Bennett said that it was "studded with gems of dialogue" and A. B. Walkley spoke of it as "one of the most fragrant first acts I know, nimbly and sweetly recommending itself to the senses." The anonymous critic of the *Graphic* wrote: "What may not be hoped for from a dramatist who can take us so far away from the conventionalities of the professional playwright, impress on the spectator with so little apparent effort the relations of his various personages, and awaken our sympathies by means so simple and so legitimate."

Henry James, sitting in the Haymarket, uncomfortably squirming at the Oscarisms, at this moment was unaware of the extent to which he had moved his audience and of the admiration he had evoked. Perhaps it was just as well.

Whatever may have been hoped for from the author of such a first act was not the act that followed. The scene was the dower house of Mrs. Domville, a villa at Richmond. The Guy Domville who faced the audience here was not the devout and noble character of the first act. He was a young man who, during the three months that elapsed between the acts, had been learning the way of the world from Lord Devenish. Clad in the costume of a dandy, full of swagger and talk of cards, the young churchman had been converted with great rapidity into a young blade addicted to the joys of good living, and embroiled now in a situation filled with intrigue.

In forsaking the simplicity of his first act Henry James had yielded to the clap-trap of artificial drama, to the *ficelle* structure of Sardou and the other dramatists he had studied with such assiduity at the Théâtre Français. He had discarded for the entire act two of his best personages, Frank Humber and Mrs. Peverel. And this after arousing a deep interest in his love story. Instead his hero had been brought face to face with a series of ill-motivated and quite irrelevant situations. The mood created by the first act was utterly destroyed.

It is no wonder that some members of the audience began to fidget; there was some coughing, and coughing in an audience under such circumstances is contagious. To no one was this clearer than to the actors themselves. We must allow for first-night nervousness, and such nervousness as existed was aggravated by the tension; it, in turn, increased the restlessness of the audience. The cool matinee idol, George Alexander, gave way to his feelings by the workings of his mouth. John Singer Sargent whispered to Graham Robertson: "Why does he open his mouth on one side like that? It makes his face all crooked."

Such tension requires but a single incident to shatter the theatre's make-believe. It came in a curious and unexpected form. Mrs. Edward Saker, in the role of the dowager Mrs. Domville, appeared in what Shaw described as a "Falstaffian make-up." She wore an elaborate gown of the period and a tall velvet hat shaped like a muff, towering on her head under nodding plumes. However accurate this costume was historically, it struck an incongruous note of caricature for a pit and gallery whose patience was being sorely tried. The critics later said that beauty had been sacrificed to strict accuracy in costume; that, however, was really beside the point. The truth was that part of the audience already had been lost to the play. A pleased audience is always willing to forgive, and is not disturbed for too long by errors in costume. But this audience was ready to titter as well as to cough. From somewhere in the back a voice yielded a line from the popular song. "Where Did You Get That Hat." Very little was required to unnerve Mrs. Saker, who was managing with some difficulty her voluminous skirt of black satin over a *panier* crinoline of huge dimensions. The impression given Graham Robertson, himself a successful costume designer, was that "the dress was particularly fine, but it wanted wearing; the huge hoop, and great black hat perched upon a little frilled undercap should have been carried by one filled with the pride of them and the consciousness of their beauty." Mrs. Saker found it difficult to have either pride or dignity. She tried instead to be self-effacing—a difficult thing with a costume that filled a large area on the stage, and with her plumes waving with every toss

of the head. Titter succeeded upon titter. The pit
and gallery became unruly, like a group of children. The audience was now participating in the
play, reaching across the footlights to the actors
instead of being reached by them—and with a
childish cruelty that mass hostility frequently as-
sumes.

Unfortunately Henry James gave further provo-
cation in his big drinking scene. James had written
Alexander that this scene could only be judged
after the test of rehearsal. It had stood that pre-
liminary test, but in the present circumstances its
feeble comedy became a glaring weakness, an element of burlesque. It is easy to see what the dramatist had intended. Years earlier, at the Théâtre
Français, he had seen Émile Augier's *L'Aventurière*
and relished the drinking scene in the second act
in which Fabrice, a clever young soldier, plies Don
Annibal with liquor in order to find out from him
the true character of Dona Clarinde, an adventuress. James's own account of this scene, and his
delight in it, shows us precisely what he wanted to
do in *Guy Domville*. "The scene was played by
Bressant and Regnier, and it has always remained
in my mind as one of the most perfect things I have
seen on the stage. The gradual action of the wine
upon Don Annibal, the delicacy with which his
deepening tipsiness was indicated, its intellectual
rather than physical manifestations, and, in the
midst of it, the fantastic conceit which made him
think that he was winding his fellow drinker round
his fingers—all this was exquisitely rendered." But
James admitted that, on the whole, drunkenness
on the stage could be "both dreary and disgusting."

With perfectly serious intent Henry James asked
of his two characters to attempt to make each other
drunk, while each was shamming drunkenness. As
actually performed there was a great deal of sur-

reptitious disposal of the drinks in flower pots—a scene which Bernard Shaw remembered in his old age and recounted many times. What was more, Alexander played it, in the words of Shaw, "with the sobriety of desperation."

The evening was lost for Henry James, but he was still at the Haymarket and spared the torment of this knowledge. A miracle was needed to save the play, and the third act, although it recaptured some of the charm of the first, did not possess miraculous qualities. The curtain rose on the interior at Porches. A solemn-looking grandfather clock presided over the room; there were white shelves built of solid wood, with quaintly designed china upon them; the doors were likewise solid, and they had genuine brass knobs. Through an open lattice one could see bright sunshine and be reminded that the charming garden of Act I lay just outside. Alexander, for all his romanticism, invariably insisted upon a maximum of reality. Nothing was left to the imagination. But the actors could no longer restore reality to their lines.

The play, nevertheless, ended on a touching and dramatically effective scene. In taking leave, Guy once again commends Mrs. Peverel to the care of Frank Humber. The last lines, with their delicate phrasing and calculated repetitions, spoken by actors less nervous and irritated than were Alexander and his cast on this night, could be extraordinarily moving.

But the audience's sympathies were not with Guy. The audience tended to agree with Devenish that Guy didn't deserve to know of Mrs. Peverel's love. *She* had won the affection of the audience and the hero was rejecting her—however noble his acceptance of the religious alternative. His sense of his vocation had been insufficiently strong when it was a question of family name and a worldly marriage; and yet it became strong when confronted with a deep and devoted love such as Mrs. Peverel's. This seemed to the greater part of the audience the height of perversity. In a James novel all this would have been explained in a way that it could not be on the stage. In the novel Henry James would have taken us into the minds of his characters and revealed to us, in particular, the nature of Guy's conflict. On the stage Guy is merely fickle, a prey to temptation, easily turned from one course to another so that we begin to doubt whether he should take holy orders without a deep re-examination of his religious feelings. To the audience his conduct could seem only capricious and arbitrary.

The most direct expression of the audience's impatience came in the temporarily hushed house when Alexander, with a great show of feeling, delivered himself of the speech: "I'm the last, my lord, of the Domvilles. . . ."

A voice from the gallery burst into the stillness. "It's a bloody good thing y'are."

## 6.

At the Haymarket, Henry James had listened to the last epigrams and to the overwhelming applause from the audience. He came out into the cold night and threaded his way through the line of carriages. He walked down the short street leading into St. James's Square, anxious, disturbed, overcome with fear. Oscar Wilde's play had struck him as helpless, crude, clumsy, feeble, vulgar. He later threw all these adjectives at it. And yet it had been accepted by the audience, accepted with eagerness, with laughter, with unstinted applause. Its success, it seemed to Henry James, could only be an ill omen for *Guy Domville*.

The thought caused him to stop in the middle of St. James's Square. He was transfixed and paralyzed "by the terror of this probability." He was afraid, he later said, to go on and learn more.

We can believe him. We can believe him because he had good reason to feel unsure of himself in the theatre. He knew the sort of play he had written; he was possessed by the anxieties of a man repeatedly rejected by a wider public of readers, repeatedly rejected by managers—and yet trying his utmost to please—a man nervous and lonely in the cold London world that closed about him that night, and through which the carriages were rolling on all sides as Piccadilly came to life at the after-theatre hour. Standing in the middle of the Square Henry James suddenly found himself asking, with a sinking heart, as he thought of Oscar's play:

"How *can* my piece do anything with a public with whom *that* is a success?" In his heart he knew the answer.

He entered the St. James's Theatre by the stage door during the last minutes of his play. On the stage Alexander had backed toward the exit, somewhat awkwardly saying to Mrs. Peverel, in slowly measured accents, "Be *keynd* to him. . . . Be good to her." By nature, H. G. Wells was to recall years later, Alexander had a long face, but "at that moment with audible defeat before him, he seemed the longest and dismallest face, all face, that I have ever seen. The slowly-closing door reduced him to a strip, a line, of perpendicular gloom."

Backstage in those hurried moments no one told Henry James of the accidents of the second act. The actors were reassuring. The curtain came down and the nervous author faced the troubled manager. Beyond the proscenium there was a great roar of applause. Then there were curtain calls and the actors were applauded. Alexander received his usual ovation. Then came a brief lull. Voices, from the stalls called, "Au-thor, author." A manager possessed of a level head would have known what to do that night. He would not have brought on Henry James. Perhaps Alexander hoped to impress the recalcitrants. Perhaps H. G. Wells was right when he speculated that a "spasm of hate for the writer" may have seized Alexander. We shall never know what prompted the actor-manager to take Henry James by the hand and lead him into the bright glare of the footlights.

What followed can be told only in the words of the man who lived through that moment. "All the forces of civilization in the house waged a battle of the most gallant, prolonged and sustained applause with the hoots and jeers and catcalls of the roughs, whose roars (like those of a cage of beasts at some infernal 'zoo') were only exacerbated . . . by the conflict. It was a cheering scene, as you may imagine, for a nervous, sensitive, author to face." And again: "I no sooner found myself in the presence of those yelling barbarians . . . and learned what could be the savagery of their disappointment that one wasn't perfectly the *same* as everything else they had ever been, than the dream and delusion of my having made a successful appeal to the cosy, childlike, naïf, domestic British imagination . . . dropped from me in the twinkling of an eye."

It seemed to some of the spectators that they stood there, the matinee idol and the author, for hours, while sections of the audience acted out the Miltonic lines,

> . . . *from innumerable tongues,*
> *A dismal universal* hiss, *the sound*
> *Of public scorn.*

It was certainly not universal in this case, but the scorn was painfully audible. And the last thing that Henry James, a long-rejected, little-read author, could face with equanimity was public scorn. Bernard Shaw, trained in the give-and-take of Hyde Park, could shout back with genial, good humor at the lone individual who hissed *Arms and the Man:* "Personally I agree with my friend in the gallery—but what can we two do against so many?" Henry James was too deeply involved in this production—personally, emotionally—to find his tongue at this crucial moment; too eager for the audience's appreciation to be scornful, as Wilde might have been, too bewildered to do what Charles Lamb had done many years before—joined in the hissing of his own play. His dark beard framed a half-open mouth, set off the pallor of the cheeks, the shocked stare that some witnesses described as "scornful coolness" and others as displaying "quiet gallantry." For a moment the applause drowned out everything. John Singer Sargent wanted to leap upon the stage to rescue his friend. It must have been a common impulse among those who knew James. Douglas Ainslie, the translator of Croce, and not a close friend of James's, relates in his memoirs a similar impulse.

Then James, in those seconds that seemed like hours, standing there white and tense, made a deprecatory gesture, a movement of the arms, a shrug of the shoulders. Alexander shifted nervously from one position to another. Then the novelist turned and fled. Alexander followed. Two members of the cast, Irene Vanbrugh and Franklyn Dyall, years afterwards said that they never forgot the expression of agony on James's face as he came into the wings. Dyall said he seemed "green with dismay."

The audience had no desire to leave. Phil Burne-Jones turned in his box and applauded in the direction of those who were booing. The answer was a new storm of hisses and catcalls. It was no longer an attack on Henry James or George Alexander. In these moments it became a war between the intel-

lectual élite, the friends, the well-wishers, and the
rowdies to whom the applause was an act of defiance. This was hardly the battle for *Hernani*.
There were no Théophile Gautiers in the audience
at the St. James's to lead a romantic revolt against
the *pérruques*. Nor was Henry James a Victor
Hugo, or the leader of a literary movement. London audiences are not addicted, by and large, to
battles over artistic ideologies such as occur with
interesting regularity in Paris theatres. This was a
strange and peculiar theatrical brawl, uncharacter-
istic of London—a sudden flare-up of anger and
spite, half-lark, half-serious. It is quite unlikely that
Henry James remembered that he himself had
once, in an article written twenty years earlier, pre-
scribed hissing for certain plays since "the deceived
spectator ought to hold in his hand some instru-
ment of respectful but uncompromising disapproval." Hissing, he had written, ceases to be brutal
when it is directed only at the play and not at the
performers. It had not occurred to him to discuss
the hissing of the authors. On this night, Henry
James joined a select company of hissed authors—
Sheridan, Goldsmith, Fielding, Coleridge, Hugo,
Scribe, Sardou, Shaw. He was qualified for member-
ship in the Parisian club of hissed authors to which
his friends Flaubert, Zola and Daudet had belonged. However, Henry James had hardly faced
the "respectful disapproval" which he himself advocated.

And Alexander? He was as unaccustomed to
such treatment as Henry James. His few years at the
St. James's had been a triumph of management and
of a sudden, an audience—one of his invariably
faithful audiences—had expressed itself with a
fierce crudity, an upsurge of hostility, that was a
blow to his pride. "Alick lost his head," said Bernard Shaw. He left Henry James in the wings and

came forward to the footlights. Now there was only applause—as if to exempt him. There were cries of "Speech, speech." A voice from beyond the footlights shouted: "T'aint your fault, gov'nor, it's a rotten play."

Alexander made his speech. He spoke slowly and with emotion. "Ladies and gentlemen: In my short career as a manager I have met with so many favors at your hands that these discordant notes tonight have hurt me very much. I can only say that we have done our very best; and if we have failed, we can only try to deserve your kindness by trying to do better in the future."

There was another flurry of applause. The incident was over. The house lights were turned on, the National Anthem was played, the audience began to disperse. The well-dressed poured into the narrow outer lobby to wait for carriages. The gallery emptied itself into dark cold streets. An unidentified American woman, a friend of Clement Scott, rushed over to him in the lobby and said: "You all ought to be ashamed of yourselves. Won't it give you a misery ever after to have to own up that you're an Englishman." The drama critic solemnly recorded the remark in his memoirs, without comment.

The evening had a brief epilogue. Henry James, following the French tradition which he had religiously observed at the Southport and London productions of *The American*, had invited members of the cast of *Guy Domville* to have supper with him. The drama within a drama that he had lived that night did not change his plans. The supper took place. The details of what occurred are lost to us. It was a private affair and, so far as we know, only a few were present. The host apparently was genial and sociable. He was tired, not having slept

for several nights, and he felt that he mingled
"poorly in the fine rich gossip of some of my
guests." But he put on a brave face. No one, he
confided to Margaret Brooke, Ranee of Sarawak,
could have suspected any dejection in his attitude.
"You would have been proud of your friend," he
told her.

## 7.

The battle that raged in the St. James's Theatre
on the night of January 5, 1895, was transferred
in the ensuing days to the press. Few critics accepted the verdict of the pit and the gallery; and
even when they did, as was the case with the *Times*,
it was to reproach George Alexander for his curtain
speech. The *Times* called it a "rueful apology."
The *Daily Chronicle* called it a "painful exhibi-
tion." The Manchester *Guardian* deplored Alexander's lack of courage in apologizing "for a play
which, whatever its ultimate fate, is certainly a
credit to his theatre and management." But it was
left to Bernard Shaw to express in vigorous language the feelings of many who sat in the *Guy
Domville* audience on that first night:

"Is it good sense to accuse Mr. Henry James of a
want of grip of the realities of life because he gives
us a hero who sacrificed his love to a strong and
noble vocation for the Church? And yet when some
unmannerly playgoer, untouched by either love or
religion, chooses to send a derisive howl from the
gallery at such a situation, we are to sorrowfully
admit, if you please, that Mr. James is no dramatist,
on the general ground that 'the drama's laws the
drama's patrons give.' Pray, which of its patrons?
—the cultivated majority who, like myself and all
the ablest of my colleagues, applauded Mr. James
on Saturday, or the handful of rowdies who
brawled at him? It is the business of the dramatic

critic to educate these dunces, not to echo them.
. . . Mr. James's dramatic authorship is valid . . .
his plays are *du théâtre* when the right people are
in the theatre."

Some of the newspapers questioned Alexander's
wisdom in bringing on Henry James when he knew
the feelings of the house. Others took an intensely
British attitude and decried the poor sportsman-
ship of the audience, especially since Henry James
was a distinguished American who, as they put it,
had done Britons the honor of making his home in
their midst. Perhaps the most interesting post mor-
tems were those of the *Westminster Gazette* and
the periodical *Today,* edited by Jerome K. Jerome,
which invited spectators to describe what had happened in the immediate areas in which they had
been seated.

The letters written to these journals gave rise to
the story that Henry James had in reality been the
victim of a cabal directed against Alexander. It was
now recalled that two ladies had sent a mysterious
and hostile telegram to Alexander just before the
production was scheduled to start. A spectator reported there were some twenty men in the gallery
and as many in the upper boxes, the "veriest
roughs" who could not possibly have paid four
shillings for their seats. Each set had a leader who
gave signals for the hooting. Drinks seem to have
been served freely between acts. They went out and
came back a little less sober each time and they
were responsible for most of the noise. One rumor
had it that these men had been hired by friends of
an actress who was said to have been slighted by
Alexander. This, however, did not explain the initial applause given Alexander.

So the stories went. On subsequent nights during
*Guy Domville's* five-week run there was no trouble.
Henry James went on the second night, choosing to

sit in the gallery. He watched a hushed house give the play a cordial reception. G. W. Smalley, the New York *Tribune's* London correspondent, who also was in the gallery that night, reported: "There was nothing there or anywhere in the house but the deepest interest and most genuine enthusiasm. . . . After the last act there was a perfect storm of applause. . . ." Alexander received many curtain calls.

One is led to the conclusion that there must have been a multiplicity of causes for the troubles of the first night. There seemed to have been "predetermined mischief," as James put it, in the audience; and the play itself—and first night accidents on stage—only contributed to the restlessness of sections of the audience. There is no evidence to show that the gallery was anti-American, or that Henry James's personality was in question. Nor is it likely that the play could have offended Catholic members of the audience. On the contrary, the Catholic critics were delighted with the piety of the work.

The critics in general were unanimous that the play was ill-motivated and that its hero was perverse and fickle—"with a strong infusion," observed the unfriendly critic of the *Times,* "of what Mr. Henry James's fellow-countrymen would call 'cussedness.'" They agreed that W. G. Elliot's overacting and the drinking scene, the fuss of the second act and the lack of clarity in the third, as well as the cumbersome and over-elaborate costuming of Mrs. Saker, had contributed to the shipwreck of the play. Yet by and large Henry James had an excellent press. Strictures were confined to Alexander's obsequious speech and to the defective second act. There was unanimous admiration for the first. A brilliant first act, however, is not a whole play, as Henry James himself very well knew; and his sense of failure did not permit him to accomplish what other less discouraged playwrights have achieved despite initial set-backs—write another play that would justify the promise of *Guy Domville*.

Reading the criticisms of the three relatively unknown drama critics* who later achieved renown, we can, after half a century, see how just was their appraisal (and note, at the same time, how distinctly, even then, they wrote in character). Shaw, as we have seen, wrote with his customary verve and acerbity. "There is no reason," he said, "why life as we find it in Mr. James's novels . . . should not be represented on the stage. If it is real to Mr. James it must be real to others." Of the dialogue he said: "Line after line comes with such a delicate turn and fall that I unhesitatingly challenge any of our popular dramatists to write a scene in verse with half the beauty of Mr. James's prose. . . . I am speaking of the delicate inflexions conveyed by the cadences of the line. . . . *Guy Domville* is a story and not a mere situation hung out on a gallows of plot. And it is a story of fine sentiment and delicate manners, with an entirely worthy and touching ending." Of Alexander's role he said: "Mr. Alexander, having been treated little better than a tailor's dummy by Mr. Wilde, Mr. Pinero, and Mr. Henry Arthur Jones successively, found himself treated as an artist by Mr. James."

H. G. Wells observed that *Guy Domville* was a "play finely conceived and beautifully written," but found the second act "tedious and impossible." "People come and go in the house unchallenged like rabbits in a warren, and it was played with singular lack of spirit." He demolished Alexander in a single sentence: "In the first act Mr. Alexander, as Guy Domville, is a didactic puritan; in the second a fine generous blade; in the third he is that

* See pp. 205-217 for the texts of these reviews.

impossible, noble, iron-grey Mr. Alexander that we have seen before."

Arnold Bennett's review was written with the same pedestrian simplicity he cultivated later in his writings for the daily press. He found the "gems of dialogue" of Act I of "too modest and serene a beauty to suit the taste of an audience accustomed to the scintillating gauds of Mr. Oscar Wilde and Mr. Henry Arthur Jones." He found the behavior of pit and gallery "quite inexplicable. The piece is assuredly not faultless—far from it, but it is so beautifully written, it contains so many exquisite scenes, it is so conscientiously and artistically acted and so lavishly staged, that the *longueurs* of the second act, one would have thought, might have been either forgiven or endured in respectful silence."

It was left to the sensitive and subtle A. B. Walkley to write the most balanced appraisal of all. Attuned to James's quality of mind he saw the irony in the public's acceptance of Wilde and its rejection of James. He wrote:

> Two plays have been produced during the past few days with widely different fortunes at their birth. One, Mr. Oscar Wilde's *Ideal Husband,* at the Haymarket, a strepitous, polychromatic, scintillant affair, dexterous as a conjuror's trick of legerdemain, clever with a cleverness so excessive as to be almost monstrous and uncanny, was received with every token of success. The other, Mr. Henry James's *Guy Domville* . . . laboriously wrought, pitched in a minor key, sometimes fuliginous, at others . . . subfuse, maladroit, teasing to the pitch of exasperation, was so despitefully used by many of the audience that the manager virtually went down on his marrow-bones and sued for pardon. Yet, of these two plays, I have not the slightest hesitation in declaring that the brilliant success is infinitely

outweighed by the ostensible failure, not merely in actual achievement, but in significance, in promise for the future. Mr. Wilde's play will not help the drama forward a single inch, nor—though that is a comparatively unimportant matter—will it in the long run, add to Mr. Wilde's reputation. Mr. James's play is a defeat out of which it is possible for many victories to spring; in gathering the enemy's spears into his heart he has made a gap through which his successors will be able to pour in triumph.

James received more mail from sympathisers and well-wishers than he had in all his years as a writer. Ellen Terry invited him to come and talk to her about doing a play; Sir George Henschel, the composer and conductor, invited him to write a libretto on a New England theme which he would set to music. James refused to do the libretto ("I am unlyrical, unmusical, unrhythmical, unmanageable") and his negotiations with Ellen Terry resulted in his writing a one-act play for her.

*Guy Domville* ran its allotted four weeks, the minimum time required to exhaust Alexander's loyal audience, and lasted an extra week that included a profitable trip to Brighton. At the end James acknowledged that "what appears largely to have enabled *Guy Domville* to go even a month is the fact that almost everyone who has been to see it at all appears to have been three or four times." And irony of ironies! On January 12 George Alexander announced that he had a new play—by Oscar Wilde! It was called *The Importance of Being Earnest*. Alexander paid Henry James the equivalent of $1,300 in royalties earned during the play's forty performances. The actor-manager lost £1,873, or almost $9,000, his investment in the expensive setting and costuming.

"There is nothing, fortunately, so dead as a dead

play—unless it be sometimes a living one," Henry wrote to William on February 22. "Oscar Wilde's farce which followed *Guy Domville* is, I believe, a great success—and with his two roaring successes running now at once he must be raking in the profits."

On the night of the closing Henry James said good-bye to the cast. Then he wrote to Elizabeth Robins: "It has been a great relief to feel that one of the most detestable incidents of my life has closed."

## VI. COMPENSATIONS AND SOLUTIONS

From Henry James's notebook, January 23, 1895:

> I take up my *own* old pen again—the pen of all my old unforgettable efforts and sacred struggles. To myself—today—I need say no more. Large and full and high the future still opens. It is now indeed that I may do the work of my life. And I will.
>
> x x x x x
>
> I have only to *face* my problems.
>
> x x x x x
>
> But all that is of the ineffable—too deep and pure for any utterance. Shrouded in sacred silence let it rest.—

### 1.

He had written to William James at the outset of his dramatic years, "I am going to attack, renewedly and repeatedly, the almost impregnable fortress of the theatre." No one had repulsed his attacks. The fortress had remained (for him) quite simply impregnable. Now, at fifty-two, he could return to the observation post of the mind he had occupied during all the long years that preceded his play-writing. Here no one would challenge him:

no manager could reject his dreams or apply the brutal axe of Excision to his manuscripts. He was the undisputed master, the omniscient observer. He could speculate, analyze, lose himself in his fancies —convert these into realities to replace the other realities that lay outside and beyond his literary monastery.

And so, immediately after *Guy Domville,* we find him dreaming self-consolatory stories, seeking "compensations and solutions." *His works were not popular?* This was because they were "too good" for the public whose "huge, flat foot" he had sought to measure. Thus he wrote a short story, "The Next Time," about an author who seeks to create potboilers, but is capable of producing only unread masterpieces. *His works were not understood?* This was because their form, their pattern, their texture was not perceived by the mole-like critics. Thus he wrote a short story, "The Figure in the Carpet," to plead for a criticism that might understand the artist's intentions. Again and again he spoke of having tried to make a "sow's ear out of a silk purse."

While he thus sought and found reassurance for himself, on a conscious level, in stories that might be termed "rationalizations," he was nevertheless stating truths that the critics of today can readily accept. He was too discriminating for the taste of his time; his art, complex, and conforming to high standards of perfection, eluded critics, who seldom can take the true measure of greatness. And there was indeed a pattern in his work, a subtle autobiographical pattern, the manner in which he wrote his life into his work. In the *order,* the *form,* the *texture,* the very names of his people and the names he gave to his books, there lay the *figure in the carpet* for those who wished to find it.

On another level of the mind—and here we skirt

more speculative areas—he was now plunged into a nightmare of fear and insecurity. To have been rejected brutally by his public amounted to a kind of personal death, and he fought against this with all the force of his manhood. Three days after *Guy Domville,* he visited the Archbishop of Canterbury, at his country seat of Addington, near London, and there, in conversation with members of his family, he described himself as a man who had "hitherto . . . seemed to himself to have been struggling in some dim water-world, bewildered and hampered by the crystal medium, and that he had suddenly got his head above the surface, with a new perspective and an unimpeded vision." Henry James thus imaged himself as one who had been drowning and who only now could begin to breathe again. A striking image for him to have used at this time, and we can watch him, through the weeks that followed, struggling against the waves that threatened to swallow him up, groping for a foothold against oblivion. Here was the death-in-life of his fantasies of the year before. The jeering audience in St. James's had reduced him to the helplessness of an unappreciated child; it had cut at the heart of his creativity. It is perhaps no coincidence that the first note he set down after *Guy Domville* was that of a tale of horror, a nightmare story, told him by the Archbishop at Addington, which became "The Turn of the Screw." He had written a few years earlier two short stories about ill-starred children; now he moved into a world of childish fear and terror. Two novels and a novelette are set down in rapid succession picturing fragile innocents, bright, precocious, blooming, worldly-wise, pushed and fenced by adult hands, doomed to early blight.

For the children of the stories he wrote at fifty-five there was no happy childhood. A child is murdered (*The Other House*); childhood is a special hell created by adults (*What Maisie Knew*); adults plague children with phantoms ("The Turn of the Screw"). The Henry James who had retreated from his older brother rather than compete with him; the celibate Henry, whose life would never be shared with his own children (whose author in "The Lesson of the Master" describes children as contributing to "damnation, artistically speaking"), dreamed tales of children assaulted by great forces of aggression. And since these dreams sprang full-blown from his mind at this climactic moment in his literary career, we must accept them as evidence of the inner disturbance provoked by his theatrical failures. He moved from his disturbed present into a disturbed childish past. It is no wonder that James described the ghostly tale as the finest form of the fairy tale. In saying this he linked the fear and wonder of his ghosts with his childhood. There had been too many preceptors and governesses, too many pushing hands in his own childhood—and apparently too many little rivals.

2.

On February 14, 1895, little more than a month after *Guy Domville,* Henry James sat down at his desk to work out the details of a story he had noted the previous year. "I have my head, thank God, full of visions. One has never too many—one has never enough. Ah, just to let one's self go—at last. . . ." He glances at the theme which was to become *The Wings of the Dove,* he goes on to glance at the note that foreshadowed *The Golden Bowl.* He expresses some worry about the "adulterine" element in this theme; it would be difficult to sell such a story to the highly sensitive American "family" magazines. The solution would lie in the handling of the sub-ject. . . . He muses, "*Voyons, voyons* may I not instantly sit down to a little close, clear full sce-

nario of it?" Suddenly at the mention of the word
*scenario* there comes an intense moment of perception:

> As I ask myself the question, *with* the very asking
> of it, and the utterance of that word [scenario] so
> charged with memories and pains, something seems to
> open out before me, and at the same time to press
> upon me with an extraordinary tenderness of embrace.
> Compensations and solutions seem to stand there with
> open arms for me—and something of the 'meaning'
> to come to me of past bitterness, of recent bitterness
> that otherwise has seemed a mere sickening, unfla-
> voured draught.

He asks himself a still more important question:

> Has a *part* of all this wasted passion and squandered
> time (of the last 5 years) been simply the precious les-
> son, taught me in that roundabout and devious, that
> cruelly expensive, way, *of the singular value for a
> narrative plan too* of the (I don't know *what* ade-
> quately to call it) divine principle of the Scenario?

If this was the case, he almost blessed the "pangs
and the pains and the miseries" of the "whole
tragic experience."

> IF there has lurked in the central core of it this ex-
> quisite truth—I almost hold my breath with suspense
> as I try to formulate it; so *much,* hangs radiantly there
> as depending on it—this exquisite truth that what I
> call the divine principle in question is a key that,
> working in the same *general* way fits the complicated
> chambers of *both* the dramatic and the narrative lock:
> IF, I say, I have crept round through long apparent
> barrenness, through suffering and sadness intolerable
> to that rare perception—why my infinite little loss is
> converted into an almost infinite little gain. The long
> figuring out, the patient, passionate little *cahier,* be-

comes the *mot de l'énigme,* the thing to live by. Let me commemorate here, in this manner, such a portentous little discovery, the discovery, probably, of a truth of real value even if I exaggerate, as I daresay I do, its *portée,* its magicality.

He did not exaggerate the importance of the "divine principle of the Scenario," for he was to come back to it again and again in the notebook entries of the remaining years. He called it also "mastery of fundamental statement," and as the months passed he grew increasingly attached to this simple device, derived from his work methods of his dramatic years: that of setting down a full outline of each project, a rough statement, a scenario, even when a trivial short story was involved. He had, in earlier days, communed with himself in his notebooks, never to any extended length. Now there appear in his scribblers full-length scenarios for his novels; this explains the detailed working out of *The Spoils of Poynton* and *What Maisie Knew* and the elaborate "Project" for *The Ambassadors* written for his publishers. "Projects" or scenarios or "rough statements" existed for all his later novels; however, after he started dictating directly to the typewriter he did not include these in his notebooks, and most of them were destroyed by him in the flames to which he consigned the bulk of his papers a few years before his death. Henry James now brought to fiction the very mechanics he had invoked for the writing of his plays. He talks of his fiction as if it were drama. "What then is it," he asks himself at one point in working out the *Spoils,* "that the rest of my second little act, as I call it . . . must do?" And he goes on: "What I feel more and more that I must arrive at, with these things, is the adequate and regular practice of some such economy of clear summarization as will *give* me from

point to point, each of my steps, stages, tints,
shades, every main joint and hinge, in its place, of
my subject—give me, in a word, my clear order and
expressed sequence. I can then *take* from the table,
successively, each fitted or fitting piece of my little
mosaic."

This is the carpenter-dramatist at work (as James
envisioned him years before) on his knees, disposing
of his goods this that and the other way, packing
his coffer in the "one way that is mathematically
right"; it is not the old-time novelist spinning a
discursive narrative, chatting, pausing to describe,
taking his reader on diverse journeys, letting his
pen run cheerfully away with him; it is the novel
given a form as calculated as a fugue or a sonata,
the boundaries defined and within them the work
built step by step in accordance with its particular
substance and logic. In his note for *The Spoils of
Poynton* from which we have quoted above, Henry
James went on to write:

> When I ask myself what there may have been to
> show for my long tribulation, my wasted years and
> patiences and pangs, of theatrical experiment, the
> answer, as I have already noted here, comes up as just
> possibly *this:* what I have gathered from it will per-
> haps have been exactly some such mastery of funda-
> mental statement—of the art and secret of it, of
> expression, of the sacred mystery of structure. Oh yes
> —the weary, woeful time has done something for me,
> has had in the depths of all its wasted piety and pas-
> sion, an intense little lesson and direction. What that
> resultant is I must now actively show. . . .

He actively showed it from then on: he attached
the utmost importance to his "subject-noting," the
"working-out" sessions, the "thinking out . . . pen
in hand." In one of his short stories ("The Death
of the Lion") he described an author's scenario as

"loose, liberal confident, it might have passed for a great gossiping eloquent letter—the overflow into talk of an artist's amorous plan."

He thus practised to the full the application to the narrative plan of his "divine principle of the Scenario"; his "patient, passionate little *cahier*" became indeed the key to his work, the *mot de l'énigme,* the figure in the carpet, "the thing to live by." He rejoiced in the elaborate mechanics of his writing—the process of fitting the scenario key, as he had put it, into the "complicated chambers of both the dramatic and narrative lock." In the process, he was equating drama and fiction, the same door and the same lock led him to both. The effect of this method on his later work remains to be fully appraised. In applying his drama-working methods to the novel he gave to his fiction the qualities of the play. His protagonists would be shown at the crucial moments in their lives, face to face with their conflicts and decisions and in scenes as carefully set as if they were the work of the stage designer and the property man. The theatre had taught him rigid economy and how to allow a situation to unfold without the intervention of the narrator; how to obtain intensity from a given situation by extracting all the elements of drama it contained. It led him also into scenic economy; those experiments in which he heightens tension by leaving out certain awaited climactic scenes, as in *The Wings of the Dove.*

3.

Henry James had arrived at the ultimate integration, in his work, of Picture and Scene. ("I realize —none too soon—that the *scenic* method is my absolute, my imperative, my *only* salvation.") The series of experiments James embarked upon led him from a group of three short, play-like novels, to the final major novels of his career which combine his qualities of analyst and painter with those of the artist of the scene, the dramatist. On the surface these later novels appear the reverse of dramatic; the situation seems to be static while we are in the minds of the Jamesian characters and observers, following them through their analyses and their problems. Each passage of analysis, however, leads invariably to a sharply-defined scene so planned as to advance and resolve the given situation—the whole arranged in a symmetrical pattern. The work possesses an organic architectural design. Background is reduced to essentials, as on the stage. The novel is stripped of trimmings and accessories.

His first novel after the dramatic years was *The Spoils of Poynton,* his second the adaption into fiction of his scenario of *The Other House.* In accomplishing this work, in which, for the first time, he consciously used a scenario designed for a play as the basis for a novel, he carried out what he had adumbrated in his notebooks. A dozen years later, in one of his outbursts of emotion in his notes, he spoke of *The Other House* as "a precedent, a support, a divine little light to walk by." He went on to write *What Maisie Knew,* "The Turn of the Screw," "In the Cage," with an ever more rigorous application of the scenario principle and the scenic structure resulting therefrom, until in *The Awkward Age* (1899) he set down an entire novel in dialogue—one scene for each of his personages and each scene illuminating the central situation. He described it as "all dramatic and scenic" and explained it as "presented episodes, architecturally combined and each making a piece of the building, with no going behind, no *telling about* the figures save by their own appearance and action." The image James used in his preface to this work was that of a series of lamps disposed around a central subject "the function of each of which would be to light with all due intensity one of its aspects."

Readers of Henry James's prefaces will recall how often he describes the manner in which a subject appealed to him, and how in each case he heard the inner voice say, "Dramatize, dramatize!" It is true that he had "dramatized" long before the dramatic years. But it was only after these years that he applied the scenic method with complete and conscious consistency. In the preface to *What Maisie Knew* he acknowledges the "inveterate instinct" with which his stories "keep conforming to the 'scenic' law" and he adds, "Going over the pages here placed together has been for me, quite to watch the scenic system at play. The treatment by 'scene' regularly, quite rhythmically recurs." He speaks elsewhere of the "charm of the scenic consistency," of "those scenic conditions which are as near an approach to the dramatic as the novel may permit itself," of "the blest operation . . . of my Dramatic principle, my law of successive Aspects."

Time and time again, seeking to reassure himself, he wondered whether the dramatic effort had really been worth while. With the passage of years the conviction grew that it had been his salvation. One day in 1895, when the hurt was still great, he wrote: "Is the beauty of all that effort—of all those unutterable hours—lost forever? Lost, lost, lost? It will take a greater patience than the others to see!" A moment before he had written, "How a click of perception . . . brings back to me all the strange sacred time of my thinking-out, this way, pen in hand, of the stuff of my little theatrical trials. The old patiences and intensities—the working of the old passion. The old problems and dimnesses—the old solutions and little findings of light. . . ."

Six years later, when he was launched in the writing of his three final novels, he set down in his notebook the germ for a story (May 23, 1901) and added: "How, after a long intermission, the charm of this little subject-noting . . . glimmers out to me again—lighting up for me something of the old divine light, rekindling the little old sacred possibilities, renewing the little link with the old sacred days. Oh, sacred days that are still somehow *there* —that it would be the golden gift and miracle, today, still to find *not* wasted!"

Eight years later he comes back to this again:

> A sense with me, divine and beautiful, of hooking on again to the 'sacred years' of the old D[e] V[ere] Gardens time, the years of the whole theatric dream and the 'working out' sessions, all ineffable and uneffaceable, that went with that, and that still live again, somehow (indeed I *know* how!) in their ashes. . . .

In retrospect the aches and pains and harsh struggles of the dramatic years slipped away and what remained was the beneficent memory of the positive good acquired in writing scenarios for his plays and working out, step by step, scene, character, action. For Henry James, the years devoted to the plays were always to be—since he now applied to the full the knowledge and method they gave him—the "strange sacred time" that had yielded the secret of "the sacred mystery of structure," the "old sacred days"—and finally "the sacred years."

4.

And thus it was that in the early morning hours of January 4, 1910, in scrawling the notes that ultimately shaped themselves into *The Ivory Tower*, Henry James set down those words which were our point of departure and to which we now can return:

> I come back yet again and again, to my only seeing it in the dramatic way—as I can only see everything and anything now. . . .

The closer he got to his "dramatic way" he told himself—by which he meant the method of the scenario and the application of the scenic method —"the closer I get to the problem of the application of it in any particular case, the more I get *into* that application, so the more doubts and torments fall away from me, the more I know where I am, the more everything spreads and shines and draws me on and I'm justified of my logic and my passion."

> *Causons, causons, mon bon*—oh celestial, soothing, sanctifying process, with all the high sane forces of the sacred time fighting, through it, on my side! Let me fumble it gently and patiently out—with fever and fidget laid to rest—as in all the old enchanted months! It only looms, it only shines and shimmers, *too* beautiful and too interesting; it only hangs there too rich and too full and with too much to give and to pay; it only presents itself too admirably and too vividly, too straight and square and vivid, as a little organic and effective Action.

"Celestial, soothing, sanctifying process!" The dramatic years—the sacred years—had yielded their full harvest, and not so much in the plays written now and some two or three the work of a later, less harried, time (although twelve plays was as substantial a number as any playwright might produce in a lifetime) as in the consequences for his fiction arising from their creation. It would be inaccurate to dismiss the plays themselves as having served only as a school of experience for the final works, the so-called "major phase." So qualified an authority as Bernard Shaw has described the earlier plays as stageworthy, while rejecting the later works as cast in a dialogue "inhumanly literary"; while, on the other hand, the no less authoritative Granville-Barker considered the later works, particularly *The Outcry,* to be as manageable as a Restoration play or a play of Chekhov's. *Guy Domville,* during its brief existence, was praised alike for its cadenced dialogue and for the human situation it dramatized. Most critics have recognized the high dramatic qualities residing in the plays, as indeed in all the work, of James.

These plays are thus more than literary curiosities. They can be read in the light of the theatre for which they were written and the audience for which they were intended, as well as in the context of Henry James's creative life. They can be read— some of them—for intrinsic merit, for some of their scenes of high comedy, for the drollery or depth of the characterizations, for the intensity of the drama. They represent in especial for students of the dramatic form, a picture of a highly-cultivated mind at grip with the problem of reproducing life within the proscenium-frame and, as James so often put it, in a civilization in which entertainment must be provided between dinner and the suburban trains. Above all they are part of a very human and a very touching story—that of a writer stumbling and searching, with obstinate passion, to win success on the stage and then, after a series of painful defeats, due in large measure to an inability to face the realities of the theatre, wresting from his failures a final and a major victory, finding in the scenic method the salvation that enabled him to pursue his fictional art and arrive at those discoveries which mark him out as one of the great architects of the modern novel.

*Paris 1932*
*New York 1948*
*Cambridge 1960*

# II

# Guy Domville

PLAY IN THREE ACTS

BY HENRY JAMES

# CHARACTERS

GUY DOMVILLE
LORD DEVENISH
FRANK HUMBER
GEORGE ROUND, *Lieutenant R.N.*
SERVANT
MRS. PEVEREL
MRS. DOMVILLE
MARY BRASIER
FANNY
MILLINERS

*Period—1780*

# GUY DOMVILLE

## ACT FIRST

*The garden of an old house in the West of England; the portion directly behind the house, away from the public approach. Towards the centre a flat old-fashioned stone slab, on a pedestal, formed like a table and constituting a sun-dial. Close to it a garden-seat. On the right a low wooden gate, leading to another part of the grounds. On the left a high garden wall with a green door. A portion of the house is visible at the back, with a doorway, a porch and a short flight of steps. A waning June afternoon. Enter* FRANK HUMBER, *by the wooden gate. Enter* FANNY *from the house.*

FANNY. You're wanted, sir! Excuse me, sir; I thought you were Mr. Domville.

FRANK. Isn't Mr. Domville in the house?

FANNY. No indeed, sir: I came out to look for him.

FRANK. He's not *that* way: I left my horse at the stable, where, I may mention, I had to put him up myself.

FANNY. I'm not afraid of beasts, sir, and if I had been there I would have taken hold of him. Peter's away with my mistress.

FRANK. And where has your mistress gone?

FANNY. Over to Taunton—in the old green gig.

125

FRANK. A plague on the old green gig! I've ridden five miles to see her.

FANNY. You often do *that,* sir!

FRANK. Not half so often as I want!

FANNY. We all know at Porches what you want, sir! (*Sympathetically.*) She'll come back to you!

FRANK. It was just in that hope I rode over!

FANNY. (*With a laugh.*) Oh, I mean back from Taunton!

FRANK. I trust so—if the gig holds out! And who is it then wants Mr. Domville?

FANNY. It is my mistress that mostly wants him, sir!—she sends me for him to this place and that. But at present he happens to have a different call. This visitor!

(*Enter* LORD DEVENISH *from the house.*)

FRANK. Leave me with him!

FANNY. (*With a curtsey to* LORD DEVENISH.) I'll try the pond—or the river, sir! (*Exit by the green door.*)

LORD DEVENISH. Does she mean to *drag* 'em? I hope he ain't drowned!

FRANK. My friend Mr. Domville has the habit of fishing, sir.

LORD DEVENISH. The most innocent of pleasures —yet perhaps the most absorbing! In Mr. Domville's apparent absence I rejoice to find myself introduced to one of his friends.

FRANK. May I inquire if *you* also enjoy that title?

LORD DEVENISH. I hope to win it, sir! I've travelled for the purpose all the way from London! My business with Mr. Domville is urgent—so urgent that while impatiently waiting, just now, till he should be summoned, I ventured to step out of the house in the hope of meeting him the sooner.

FRANK. Under the impression that he *lives* at Porches?

LORD DEVENISH. That impression has already been

corrected. A modest habitation in the village was pointed out to me on my arrival.

FRANK. Mr. Domville's humble lodging—at the baker's.

LORD DEVENISH. I smelt the warm bread a mile off! I had the privilege of an interview with the baker's wife, and it was in consequence of the information she gave me that I knocked without delay at *this* door.

FRANK. Mr. Domville spends most of his time here.

LORD DEVENISH. A charming place—to spend most of one's time!

FRANK. That depends on what one spends it in!

LORD DEVENISH. *Mine* must all go to business— business of marked importance.

FRANK. A matter, evidently, of life and death!

LORD DEVENISH. You may judge, sir, that I haven't posted night and day for a trifle! I learned from the baker's wife that Mr. Domville *does* come home to bed: but the nature of my errand forbade me to wait till he should happen to be sleepy. I stand engaged, moreover, not to let Mr. Domville slip.

FRANK. I may let you know, then, that you've arrived in the nick of time! He goes to-morrow.

LORD DEVENISH. (*Startled.*) Goes where?

FRANK. Into retreat, as we Catholics call it.

LORD DEVENISH. (*Raising his hat.*) The true and only Church!

FRANK. (*Gratified.*) You're one of us, sir?

LORD DEVENISH. The blackest sheep in the fold!

FRANK. The fold here is very small. But we're protected by my Lord Edenbrook.

LORD DEVENISH. He provides, I know, for your spiritual nourishment.

FRANK. His private chapel, his worthy chaplain, are precious comforts to us.

LORD DEVENISH. The centre, of course, of your

little cluster of the faithful. Why then should Mr. Domville forsake such privileges?

FRANK. For the sake of others that are greater. To enter a religious house.

LORD DEVENISH. As a preparation for holy orders?

FRANK. The time for his ordination has at last come. He starts in the morning for Bristol.

LORD DEVENISH. Thank God, then, I swore at the postboys! He takes ship for France?

FRANK. For Douai and the good Fathers who brought him up, and who tried, heaven reward them! to do the same by *me!*

LORD DEVENISH. The Benedictines? You were both at school with them?

FRANK. A part of the time together. But *I'm* not of the stuff of which churchmen are made!

LORD DEVENISH. And you consider that Mr. Domville *is?*

FRANK. It's not I—it's everyone. He has what they call the vocation.

LORD DEVENISH. Then have I come too late? (*Re-enter* FANNY *from the green door.*) Can't you find him?

FANNY. Not by the water, sir. But the dairy-maid has seen him: he's gone to walk with the little master.

FRANK. The little master's the little pupil.

LORD DEVENISH. Mrs. Peverel's son?

FRANK. Her only one—poor little fatherless imp! Guy Domville, recommended to her by Lord Eden-brook's chaplain, has had for the last year the happiness of being his tutor. Thank you, Fanny. We'll wait.

(*Exit* FANNY *to the house.*)

LORD DEVENISH. Your own preference, sir, is to stay?

FRANK. Assuredly—when I've ridden five miles to take leave of him.

LORD DEVENISH. At so private an interview with so old a friend my presence will perhaps be indiscreet. May I therefore ask you to be so good as to make it clear to him that I await him impatiently at the inn?

FRANK. I shall be able to make it clearer if I'm permitted to mention your name.

LORD DEVENISH. (*Drawing from the breast of his waistcoat a letter without a seal.*) My name is on this letter, which expresses the importance of my mission and which I have been requested to place in his hand. He will receive it, however, with deeper concern from yours.

FRANK. (*With the letter.*) He shall have it as soon as he returns. (*Indicating the wooden gate.*) That's the short way to the village.

LORD DEVENISH. Before I go may I ask you another? Is Mrs. Peverel of the Sussex Peverels?

FRANK. Her late husband was of that famly. She's a niece of my Lord Edenbrook.

LORD DEVENISH. Very good blood! And a widow of some—antiquity?

FRANK. Antiquity? Why she's just *my* age!

LORD DEVENISH. (*Laughing.*) The very flower of youth!—And very charming?

FRANK. Judge for yourself, sir!

(*Enter* MRS. PEVEREL *from the house.* LORD DEVENISH, *removing his hat, remains a moment meeting her eyes while she returns his look. Then he makes a ceremonious bow and goes out by the wooden gate.*)

MRS. PEVEREL. (*Surprised.*) What does the gentleman desire?

FRANK. To have speech our young divine.

MRS. PEVEREL. Pray, who *is* he?

FRANK. I believe that letter tells.

MRS. PEVEREL. (*With the letter.*) "For Mr. Domville, introducing my Lord Devenish."

FRANK. (*Surprised.*) My Lord Devenish?

MRS. PEVEREL. (*Wondering.*) Isn't that the name —the name—?

FRANK. The name of a nobleman of extraordinary assurance!

MRS. PEVEREL. That's just what I mean—the one who was said to be Mrs. Domville's great adorer.

FRANK. Do you mean the lady's lover? I never knew any Mrs. Domville but the mother of our good friend.

MRS. PEVEREL. I speak of the widow of one of his kinsmen—the one that was the head of the family.

FRANK. (*Smiling.*) He's not the head of *ours!* God bless you for such a letter!

MRS. PEVEREL. (*Turning over* LORD DEVENISH'S *letter.*) It's not sealed, you see. (*Absent.*) What does he want of Mr. Domville?

FRANK. I don't mean *that* one—I mean *yours,* that came yesterday. You see it has brought me over.

MRS. PEVEREL. Didn't you come over to see your friend?

FRANK. *You're* my friend, and when I come to your house you're always the person I come for! Especially when you let me know that you desire it.

MRS. PEVEREL. (*Surprised.*) Is that what my letter conveyed?

FRANK. It conveyed that I might ride over if I liked—which comes to the same thing. And it conveyed some other things. Have you already forgotten?

MRS. PEVEREL. I don't remember—I'm miserably sad. We're losing our best company.

FRANK. Dear lady, it's you who are mine, and I haven't lost you yet!

MRS. PEVEREL. You haven't yet gained me, Mr. Humber!

FRANK. What then did your letter mean?

MRS. PEVEREL. I don't know *what* it meant! I'll tell you some other time!

FRANK. Thank you for that. I assure you I look forward to other times.

MRS. PEVEREL. Oh, we shall have leisure! It stretches out like the Great Desert! The cruel loss will be Geordie's. He parts with his comrade—with his idol!

FRANK. The child loves him so?

MRS. PEVEREL. Loves him? He clings to him—he's spending his last hour with him! Such devotion as my boy has enjoyed and such perfect tenderness— such an influence and such an example! And now it all goes!

FRANK. It goes to a greater work!

MRS. PEVEREL. (*Musing, with a vague shrug.*) Yes, yes—a greater work!

FRANK. He'll rise to high honours—be one of the Princes of the Church.

MRS. PEVEREL. I don't know if he'll be one of its "Princes"—but he may very well be one of its Saints.

FRANK. (*Laughing.*) Ah, *that's* more difficult! for that you must give up things!

MRS. PEVEREL. (*With decision.*) Well—he'll give them up! He's one of those who *can!*

FRANK. Dear lady, your boy loses one friend, but he keeps another! I don't compare myself—except for the interest I may take—with such a companion, with such a benefactor as Guy. I'm not clever, I'm not learned, I shall never rise to honours, much less to holiness! But I can stand firm—I can keep watch —I can take his little hand in mine. Mrs. Peverel, let *me* be something to him!

MRS. PEVEREL. You can be as good-natured as you like—my house is always open to you. What more do you want?

FRANK. You know what I want—what I've

wanted these two years. I've taken you on this side and on that, but you always have some side that's turned away. Haven't I gone all round you *yet*?

MRS. PEVEREL. (*Smiling.*) You talk as if you were buying a horse!

FRANK. I'd buy fifty, if you'd sit behind 'em! Let me stand to-day on the ground we just spoke of! Let your affection and your anxieties be mine. Let your boy be *my* boy!

MRS. PEVEREL. (*As if consentingly, resignedly.*) Well—he has given you a bit of his heart.

FRANK. He's a fine example to his mother!

MRS. PEVEREL. Remain then in his good graces! They ought to be back. He'll be very tired.

FRANK. (*Smiling.*) With *me* he needn't fear that!

MRS. PEVEREL. I'm speaking of Mr. Domville.

FRANK. *I'm* speaking, dear lady, of myself! You haven't admitted me at last only to put me off once more? What did your good words mean if they didn't mean that I should at last have my answer?

MRS. PEVEREL. You shall have it tomorrow.

FRANK. (*Gravely impatient.*) Ah, you don't treat me well!

MRS. PEVEREL. (*As if admitting this, conciliatory.*) You shall have it to-night!

FRANK. Why not now?

MRS. PEVEREL. Give me this last hour! (*Then in a totally different tone and as if forcibly to change the subject, while she draws from her pocket a very small box, from which she removes the cover.*) What do you think of that?

FRANK. (*With the box, pleased, interested.*) A fine gem, an intaglio?

MRS. PEVEREL. A precious antique that belonged to my father. I made the goldsmith at Taunton set it as a seal.

FRANK. And you went over to get it?

MRS. PEVEREL. For a gift at parting.

FRANK. (*Disconcerted.*) At parting?

MRS. PEVEREL. With Mr. Domville.

FRANK. (*Ruefully.*) Oh! (*Gives her back the box and turns away.*) Here he is to receive it!

(*Enter* GUY DOMVILLE *from the house.*)

GUY. We went further than we knew and Geordie's a little lame. It's nothing—I think his shoe wasn't right and that it will pass before morning. But I've sent him to bed and told him I would ask you to go to him.

MRS. PEVEREL. (*Very prompt.*) I'll go to him!

GUY. I'll wait for you here.

(*Exit* MRS. PEVEREL *to the house.*)

FRANK. You can't do that when you're waited for yourself.

GUY. Waited for—by whom?

FRANK. That letter will tell you.

GUY. (*With the letter; vague.*) "My Lord Devenish"?

FRANK. He's cooling his heels at the inn.

GUY. (*Reading.*) "Dear and honoured kinsman: This is to entreat you to give such welcome as is fitting to our noble friend, my trusty messenger, the Lord Devenish, and lend a patient ear to all he will say to you—much better than she herself can —for your loving cousin and humble servant Maria Domville." (*Vaguely recalling.*) She must be the widow of my cousin who died ten years ago.

FRANK. And the reputed mistress of her noble friend?

GUY. (*Disconcerted.*) His reputed mistress?

FRANK. (*Laughing.*) Pardon me, Guy—I forgot your cloth!

GUY. I'm not of the cloth yet!

FRANK. You might be, with your black clothes and your shy looks: such an air of the cold college —almost of the cold cloister! Will you go to his lordship? He's counting the minutes.

GUY. (*Hesitating, glancing at his letter again.*) "A patient ear"?—I must take leave of Mrs. Peverel first.

FRANK. Can't you do that later?

GUY. Not if my visitor's to command me and the coach is to start at dawn.

FRANK. Then *I* mustn't take your time!

GUY. Be easy, dear Frank. We're old, old friends. You must let me tell you how often I shall think of you and how much happiness I wish you.

FRANK. Do you remember, when you say that, the happiness I must long for?

GUY. I remember it. I desire it.

FRANK. You speak out of your goodness!

GUY. Out of our long affection—yours and mine.

FRANK. I can remember as far back as your mother, and the wonder with which I listened when she told me that you were to be bred up a priest.

GUY. God rest her pure spirit—it was an honest vow! The vow has been fulfilled!

FRANK. You must help me to fulfil mine—I think you can.

GUY. I shall always be glad to help you.

FRANK. I mean now—on the spot—before you're lost to us. You go for years, I suppose; perhaps even forever.

GUY. Yes; perhaps even for ever! I give up my life—I accept my fate.

FRANK. (*Laughing.*) You're not dead yet! But for *us*—it *is* your last hour.

GUY. My last! My *last!* I must therefore do something very good with it. *How* can I help you, Frank?

FRANK. By speaking for me—by telling her to *believe* in me. She thinks all the world of you.

GUY. She's attached to our holy Church.

FRANK. That's just what I mean. Your thoughts are not as other men's thoughts: your words are not as other men's words. It's to a certain extent her duty to act on them, so you're the man of all men to plead my cause.

GUY. (*After a moment.*) Will you be very good to her?

FRANK. I give you my word before heaven.

GUY. Some men—are not gentle. And *she*—she's *all* gentleness!

FRANK. Oh, I know what she is!

GUY. Then you'll be faithful, tender, true?

FRANK. My dear man, I worship the ground she treads on! And I've a good estate and an ancient name.

GUY. (*After a moment.*) I'll plead your cause.

FRANK. Now, then, is your time!

(*Re-enter* MRS. PEVEREL.)

MRS. PEVEREL. The child's only tired—but he's very wide awake. He wants to hug you again!

GUY. I'll go and be hugged!

MRS. PEVEREL. Not yet—he'll be quieter. (*To* HUMBER.) You've ridden far enough to deserve refreshment. They've put some out in the White Parlour.

FRANK. I'll drink to Domville's preferment! (*Exit to the house.*)

GUY. He worships the ground you tread on, and he swears before heaven he'll be good to you.

MRS. PEVEREL. (*Smiling.*) Did he ask you to tell me so?

GUY. And he has a good estate and an ancient name.

MRS. PEVEREL. Not so ancient as yours, my friend —one of the two or three oldest in the kingdom!

GUY. Oh, I'm giving up my name! I shall take another!

MRS. PEVEREL. You have indeed the vocation, Mr. Domville.

GUY. I have the opportunity. I've lived with my eyes on it, and I'm not afraid. The relinquished ease—the definite duties—the service of the Church —the praise of God: these things seem to wait for me! And then there are people everywhere to help.

Mrs. Peverel. If you help others as you've helped me, your comfort will indeed be great!

Guy. I *have* my comfort, for under your roof I've found—my only way, my deepest need. I've learned here what I am—I've learned here what I'm not. Just now, as I went from place to place with the child, certain moments, certain memories came back to me. I took him the round of all our rambles, yours and mine—I talked to him prodigiously of his mother.

Mrs. Peverel. *I* shall talk to him of his absent tutor.

Guy. Talk of me sometimes with Frank Humber!

Mrs. Peverel. (*Abrupt, irrelevant, with her eyes on the letter that lies on the stone.*) Who's my Lord Devenish?

Guy. (*Startled.*) I ought to go and learn!

Mrs. Peverel. Doesn't your letter tell you?

Guy. Read it, and you'll see.

Mrs. Peverel. I won't read it—thank you!

Guy. He *will* be very good to you.

Mrs. Peverel. Of whom are you speaking?

Guy. Of Frank Humber. He'll help you—he'll guard you—he'll cherish you. Make him happy.

Mrs. Peverel. That's easily said!

Guy. Marry him!

Mrs. Peverel. Why do *you* speak of marriage, Mr. Domville?

Guy. I, the first law of whose profession, the rigid rule of whose life, is to abstain from it? I don't speak of it as a man of the world—I speak of it as a priest. There are cases in which our Mother-Church enjoins it. We must bow to our Mother-Church. (*Exit to the house.*)

MRS. PEVEREL. (*Alone.*) To bow to our Mother-Church? Am I *not* bowing to her—down to the very earth? (*Restless, nervous, she once more turns her eyes to the open letter on the table, and, taking it up with decision, stands reading it.* LORD DEVENISH *meanwhile reappears at the wooden gate and remains unperceived by her, watching her.* Re-enter LORD DEVENISH.) You're impatient, my lord.

LORD DEVENISH. (*Smiling and indicating the letter.*) Not more so than *you*, Madam!

MRS. PEVEREL. With Mr. Domville's permission.

LORD DEVENISH. My license for returning is almost as good—my insurmountable anxiety! That anxiety came into being when, in the act of retiring from this spot, I had the honour to see you face to face. It suggested reflections, and I may as well confess frankly that it forbade my going back to the inn. It keeps me at my post!

MRS. PEVEREL. I don't understand you, my lord.

LORD DEVENISH. You probably will—when Mr. Domville does!

MRS. PEVEREL. I'll send him to you—and give orders for your lordship's entertainment! (*Exit to the house.*)

LORD DEVENISH. There's no such entertainment as the presence of a charming woman! If he gave her the letter she's exactly what I seemed to guess—his confidant, his counsellor. In that case I smell contradiction! (*Enter* GUY DOMVILLE *from the house.*) But *this* fellow is worth a pass or two!

GUY. I was on the point of waiting on your lordship.

LORD DEVENISH. I've come so far to see you, sir, that I made no scruple of a few steps more. My visit has, of course, an explanation.

GUY. I receive indeed so *few*—!

LORD DEVENISH. It only lies with yourself, sir,

to be surrounded with the homage of multitudes!

GUY. You're ignorant, probably, how little, my lord, things lie with myself!

LORD DEVENISH. On the contrary, sir—it was just that knowledge that brought me hither in person, and brought me so fast. My credentials, as you've assured yourself, testify to the importance of my errand.

GUY. Mrs. Domville does me unexpected honour.

LORD DEVENISH. Not as much as you'll do *me,* sir, if you'll give me your best attention. Be seated, I pray you. It's my painful duty to begin with announcing to you the death of your nearest kinsman —your only one, the late Mr. Domville of Gaye. His horse has broken his neck for him—he was mostly too drunk to ride!

GUY. I could have wished him a more edifying end!

LORD DEVENISH. You might have wished him a seemlier life—and a little less numerous progeny! He never married.

GUY. (*Surprised.*) Yet he had children?

LORD DEVENISH. They're not worth speaking of!

GUY. Surely they're worth commiserating!

LORD DEVENISH. For losing the estate?

GUY. (*Still more surprised.*) *Do* they lose it?

LORD DEVENISH. It's shrunken, it's burdened, the old domain of Gaye, but it has stood there from the Conquest, sir, and it has never been out of your family.

GUY. But if the late Mr. Domville's children *are* my family—?

LORD DEVENISH. (*Scandalised.*) *They*—a pack of village bastards?

GUY. (*Bewildered.*) Yet if there's no one else—?

LORD DEVENISH. If there had been no one else, Mr. Domville (*ruefully feeling his loins*), I wouldn't have posted till I ached! You yourself, sir, are your family.

Guy. (*As if roused from a dream.*) I?

Lord Devenish. You're the next in succession—you're the master of Gaye.

Guy. (*Stupefied.*) I?

Lord Devenish. The heir of your kinsman, the last of your name.

Guy. (*Dazed.*) To *me,* my lord, such things are fables!

Lord Devenish. That's exactly why I came to announce them. You mightn't take 'em in from another!

Guy. I've chosen my part, my lord. I go to-morrow to take it.

Lord Devenish. The purpose of my visit, sir, is to protest against your going. Your duty is nearer at hand—it's first to the name you bear. Your life, my dear sir, is not your own to give up. It belongs to your position—to your dignity—to your race.

Guy. (*Quietly, firmly.*) I was bred up, my lord, to be a priest.

Lord Devenish. You were not bred up, I suppose, not to be a Domville!

Guy. The very Domville that, in our branch, was always given to the Church! As long ago as I remember, the Church had accepted the gift. It's too late to take it back.

Lord Devenish. Too late? Not by several hours! Your coldness seems to remind me that to your consecrated character there are images unsuitable, forbidden! Do me the favour, then, to suppose that character a moment discontinued. (*Laughing.*) Do you owe your ferocity to Mrs. Peverel?

Guy. (*Surprised, slightly resentful.*) Mrs. Peverel has been my kindest friend—she approves for me of the religious life.

LORD DEVENISH. And her way of showing her approval has been to hurry you off to Bristol?

GUY. She has not "hurried" me, my lord—she has even, from day to day, detained me.

LORD DEVENISH. (*Struck, dryly.*) Ah!—Thank heaven for that detention!

GUY. For the sake, you know, of my pupil.

LORD DEVENISH. Thank heaven for your pupil!— Have your pupil, and your pupil's mother, sir, never opened your eyes to *another* possible life—the natural, the liberal, the agreeable, the life of the world of men—and of women—in which your name gives you a place? I put you that question for Mrs. Domville.

GUY. Mrs. Domville's inquiries are a wondrous civility to a person she has never seen.

LORD DEVENISH. Let me express to him, without reserve, the extravagance of her wish to see him! When she married into your family, sir, into which she brought a very handsome accession, it was with a great zeal to serve it and to contribute, if might be, to its duration. Your kinsman who died last week succeeded to his nephew, that only son whom, in his early childhood, Mrs. Domville had the bitterness to lose. She has been twice a widow, and she has from her first marriage an amiable daughter, a consolation imperfect indeed, however prized, for the great affliction of her life.

GUY. The death of the boy you speak of?

LORD DEVENISH. The heir to your name, dear sir, the tender hope, as it then seemed, the little opening flower of your race.

GUY. When the flower was gathered the race was doomed!

LORD DEVENISH. Doomed? Not to such easy extinction! Don't you feel the long past in your blood, and the voice of the future in your ears?—You hold in your hand, sir, the generations to come!

GUY. (*Much shaken.*) What is it then, my lord—what is it you want to *do* with me?

LORD DEVENISH. To carry you to-night to your kinswoman. She has paramount things to say to you.

GUY. I ask nothing of this lady but to let me lead my life!

LORD DEVENISH. Exactly what she wants you to do! She only wants to show you *how* and to see you face to face.

GUY. I doubt if you measure, my lord, I doubt if Mrs. Domville measures, so large a sacrifice, to considerations never yet present to me—to everything I've learned to put away.

LORD DEVENISH. If you've learned to put away your proper pride, you've learnt a very ill lesson!

GUY. I know no pride so proper as that of the office I've been appointed to fill.

LORD DEVENISH. The office to which you have been appointed is that of a gallant gentleman, and the place in which to fill it is the brave old house of your fathers! Do as they did in *their* day—make it ring with the voices of children! The more little Domvilles the more good Catholics! Do what you can for *them,* and you'll do quite enough for your Church!

GUY. Break with all the past, and break with it this minute?—turn back from the threshold, take my hand from the plough?—The hour is too troubled, your news too strange, your summons too sudden!

LORD DEVENISH. I reckoned on your great understanding, sir, and the fine effect of your studies! If *before* our meeting, sir, I attached a price to your person, that price has doubled since I've had the honour to converse with you! Your place in the world was in my eye—but at present I see how you'd adorn it!

Guy. I've *no* place in the world!

Lord Devenish. I'll take leave of you on the spot, sir, if you'll declare to me, on your honour, that you're dead to the pleasures of life. I shall be happy to introduce you to them all! Can't you figure them, as a gentleman? Remember, for God's sake, that you *are* one! Stand forth like one—one of the first, as you may be, in England! That character's a treasure that you can't throw away at your will! Your kinsman, just dead, dipped it woefully into the mire. Pick it up, and brush it off, and wear it!

Guy. Who *are* you, what *are* you, my lord, that you have come here to trouble me—to tempt me?

Lord Devenish. (*Smiling.*) To "tempt" you? Thank you, sir, for that word! The world is wide— and youth is short—and opportunity shorter!

Guy. Those are exactly reasons for my leaving your lordship this instant.

Lord Devenish. Life is sweet, and friends are fond, and love—well, love is everything! (*Re-enter* Mrs. Peverel *from the house. Aside.*) *He has* it here under his nose! You come to rescue Mr. Domville from my clutches?

Mrs. Peverel. I come to beg your lordship to have patience with my country larder.

Lord Devenish. If my appetite is undeniably great, Madam, your hospitality is evidently greater!

Mrs. Peverel. Its very modest effort awaits you in the White Parlour, with Mr. Humber, whom you have already met, I think, eager to do you the honours.

Lord Devenish. (*After looking a moment from* Mrs. Peverel *to* Guy.) Put your case to Mrs. Peverel, sir. I leave him, Madam, in your hands! (*Exit to the house.*)

Guy. Who *is* he, Madam—*what* is he, that he comes here to draw me off?

MRS. PEVEREL. To draw you off?

GUY. My cousin is dead—there are no other kin —and I'm sole heir to the old estate, to the old honours, to all the duties and charges. I'm lord of the Manor of Gaye!

MRS. PEVEREL. (*With great and joyous emotion.*) What news, my friend—what news! It makes my heart beat high!

GUY. I'm sole of all our line, I'm sole of all our name.

MRS. PEVEREL. It has come to you, this way, in an instant, sought you out and taken you by the hand? Then God be praised for *your* life—since he has taken to himself the others!

GUY. And hasn't he taken *mine*—haven't I given it up to him?

MRS. PEVEREL. (*Embarrassed but for an instant.*) Given it up—yes, partly! But a priest may inherit property!

GUY. He may do good with it—yes. He may devote it to the poor—he may offer it to the Church!

MRS. PEVEREL. (*Smiling.*) He may even, without sin, keep a little of it for himself! Is the property great? shall you be rich?

GUY. God forbid me riches! The domain is shrunken and burdened. But such as it is, what they want of me is to keep everything for myself.

MRS. PEVEREL. What "they" want of you? Who are "they," if they be all dead?

GUY. Mrs. Domville's alive, and she has a plan. She clings to the name—she wants to keep it up. She has sent his lordship with the tidings.

MRS. PEVEREL. I could love his lordship for coming!

GUY. I could hate him—for coming to-night! To-morrow he'd just have missed me.

MRS. PEVEREL. But sure the lawyers would have

caught you. They'd easily have followed you to France.

GUY. It's not the lawyers that trouble me!

MRS. PEVEREL. What is it then, Mr. Domville?

GUY. It's the vision of such a change, the startling voice of such an injunction! That of my forefathers' name—which has lasted from century to century!

MRS. PEVEREL. Ah yes—the command to wear it—to wear it with honour and do great things for it!

GUY. To preserving an old, old name—to giving it to others that they, in their turn, may give it!

MRS. PEVEREL. (*Excitedly.*) They want you to *marry?*

GUY. They want me to marry.

MRS. PEVEREL. (*Eager.*) Not to marry *her?*

GUY. Her?

MRS. PEVEREL. Mrs. Domville—your cousin!

GUY. Why, she's fifty years old!

MRS. PEVEREL. (*Prompt.*) I daresay she's sixty! Then it's their simple duty—to plead for your name.

GUY. I don't care a button for my name!

MRS. PEVEREL. You do, you *do*—you've often told me so! (*In an edifying tone.*) Such a name as yours is a vast obligation!

GUY. Too great—too great for *me* to carry!

MRS. PEVEREL. *Why* too great, when you're young, when you're strong, when you've a boundless life before you?

GUY. The life I have before me is not that life —the life I have before me is simply my greater duty.

MRS. PEVEREL. Your greater duty is to listen to such a call!

GUY. Half-an-hour ago you uttered different words—words that were sweet to me about the office of which I was to enter!

MRS. PEVEREL. I uttered different words because I spoke of different things!—Half-an-hour ago everything wasn't changed!

GUY. How can everything change when my heart remains the same?

MRS. PEVEREL. Are you very sure of your heart?

GUY. No, I'm not sure! Therefore I go to-night to Bristol and Father Murray. I won't wait till the morning.

MRS. PEVEREL. (*Pleading.*) You'll give up—in one minute—so great a tradition? You'll cast away something precious as if it were something mean? Life is good, Mr. Domville: you said so and you know it.

GUY. Then why have you always spoken of renouncement?

MRS. PEVEREL. (*Smiling.*) Because, when I did so, there was nothing to renounce! Now there's too much—ask Mrs. Domville! You'll hear from her, as the lawyers say, of something to your advantage.

GUY. What advantage is like the advantage of keeping faith with one's vows?

MRS. PEVEREL. What vows do you speak of? You've taken no vows.

GUY. Not in form perhaps—I haven't burnt my ships. But the irrevocable words are seated on my lips. What has my life been but a preparation?

MRS. PEVEREL. For this—perhaps: for just this hour! To choose with understanding—to act with knowledge—to live in the world with importance!

GUY. (*Sad and ironical.*) You talk of the "world," my friend; but what do you *know* of the world?

MRS. PEVEREL. Little enough—in this country nook! But I should like to hear of it—from *you!*

GUY. I'll tell you—when I come back—everything that's base and ill of it.

Mrs. Peverel. (*Catching at this.*) Yes—when you come back!

Guy. Then everything I shall say of it will show you that *we* are safer! (*Then still nervously, restlessly irreconcileable.*) But what will Father Murray say to so black a desertion?

Mrs. Peverel. He'll say you obeyed a much clearer call. I'll despatch him a quick messenger— I'll make your reasons good to him.

Guy. If they could only be good to *me!* But they're mixed with wild thoughts and desires! Things I can't tell you—words I can't speak!

Mrs. Peverel. (*Soothing, encouraging.*) Be yourself, be your generous self, and all will be straight and smooth to you!

Guy. "Myself"—the self of yesterday? I seem suddenly to have lost it for ever!

Mrs. Peverel. Then God be praised! (*Eagerly.*) May I tell him you'll *go* with him?

Guy. (*Breaking and stopping short.*) Mrs. Peverel!—

Mrs. Peverel. (*Nervously wondering and waiting.*) How can I help you?—what can I say to you?

Guy. How much of your friendship may I ask— how much of your help may I take?

Mrs. Peverel. You may ask anything—you may take all!

Guy. (*Surprised, agitated.*) All? (*Then as he sees* Frank.) All that *he* doesn't want!

(*Re-enter* Frank Humber *from the house.*)

Frank. (*Excited, delighted, ironical.*) Here's a fine pother, you rascal—with your reverence going to Court!

Mrs. Peverel. (*Affected by the interruption, coldly.*) You've heard it from his lordship?

Frank. His lordship counts on a fresh start and a long day's run for the Domvilles! And I, my dear

lad, I pat you on the back! But you look as white
as my Yorkshire colt. (*Mystified by* Guy's *look
and appealing, as if scandalised, to* Mrs. Peverel.)
You don't mean to say he won't *take* it?

Mrs. Peverel. Mr. Domville starts for London
—to-morrow very early.

Frank. (*Elated, sympathetic.*) Shall I go and let
his lordship know?

Guy. Thank you, Frank, you can leave it to *me!*

Frank. So much the better—I've something to
say to Mrs. Peverel.

Mrs. Peverel. (*Disconcerted.*) What you have to
say had better wait, Mr. Humber.

Frank. Oh, not *again!* (*Confident, but sarcastic.*)
Why not send me home at once?

Mrs. Peverel. It's much the safest place for you!

Frank. I call on you to witness, Guy, how cruelly
she treats me!

Mrs. Peverel. She treats you beautifully when
she drives four miles for you. (*With her eyes on*
Guy; *producing the box.*) To bring you an old
gem that I've had set as a seal.

Frank. (*Delighted.*) Then it *is* for *me?*

Mrs. Peverel. It's for *you!*

Frank. (*With the box.*) How can I thank you
enough?

Mrs. Peverel. (*Dryly.*) Don't thank me too
much! (*To* Guy.) Won't you relieve his lordship?

Guy. (*Rousing himself, with loud emphasis, from
what he has just observed.*) I'll relieve him. I'll
accommodate him! (*With a complete transforma-
tion and a passionate flourish.*) Long, long live the
Domvilles!—Away, away for London! (*Exit to the
house.*)

Mrs. Peverel. (*Surrendering herself to her joy.*)
He's free—he's free!

Frank. (*Disconcerted, detached.*) "Free"? Oh, I
see. Well, so am *I*, you know; and there's other

news in the air; the good news you promised, an hour ago, on this spot, to give me in your gracious answer.

MRS. PEVEREL. I can't give it now—it's impossible; please don't *ask* me.

FRANK. (*Dismayed.*) Not "ask" you when I've been counting the minutes—not "ask" you when you've given me your word?.

MRS. PEVEREL. I've given you *no* word!—I beseech you to leave me.

FRANK. (*Bewildered, astounded.*) Then my patience that you were to reward, and this present that you've just pressed on me—?

MRS. PEVEREL. (*Impatient, brusque, eager only to get rid of him.*) I'm sorry—but your patience is wasted. I'm sorry—but the present is nothing.— It's a gift at parting.

FRANK. (*Horrified.*) You mean you *refuse* me?

MRS. PEVEREL. Utterly, Mr. Humber! And don't return to the question again!

FRANK. (*Angry.*) *That's* the sweet answer you've kept me waiting for?

MRS. PEVEREL. I couldn't give it before. But it's positive *now!*

FRANK. (*Staring.*) What's the riddle of "now"?

MRS. PEVEREL. It's not a riddle—but it's a different matter. (*Summarily.*) Good-bye!

FRANK. Where on earth's the difference? (*Then divining; overwhelmed.*) By all that's monstrous— you love *him!*

MRS. PEVEREL. (*Vehemently brushing away the charge, waving away his presence.*) Don't speak to me—don't look at me—only *leave* me! (*Almost imperiously.*) Good-bye!

FRANK. (*Pulling himself up short, making a violent effort.*) Good-bye!

(*Re-enter* LORD DEVENISH *from the house.*

*Exit* FRANK *by the wooden gate.*)

LORD DEVENISH. (*Sarcastic.*) I'm sorry you're losing your friend!

MRS. PEVEREL. (*Who has not seen him; startled, confused.*) Mr. Humber?

LORD DEVENISH. (*Amused.*) Mr. Humber as well? You'll be lonely!

MRS. PEVEREL. (*Mystified by his manner, resenting his familiarity.*) My lord—!

LORD DEVENISH. It's Mr. Domville's last minute, and I'm not sure you'll see him henceforth. We've particular need of him, in another place,* to lead a young lady to the altar: Mrs. Domville's daughter by her first marriage, the amiable and virtuous Miss Brasier; a bride in a thousand—a Catholic, a beauty, and a fortune. (*Seeing* DOMVILLE.) Long, *long* live the Domvilles!

(*Re-enter* DOMVILLE *from the house.*)

GUY. I leave you to your happiness.

LORD DEVENISH. You couldn't leave a lady at a properer moment.—It's time we *should* leave her. Come, come!

GUY. Long, long live the Domvilles!

> *Passage between* GUY *and* MRS. PEVEREL.
> *Exit* GUY *and* LORD DEVENISH. MRS. PEVEREL *alone.*

* The Huntington Library prompt-book contains an inserted speech here for Mrs. Peverel. She echoes: "Particular need!"

# ACT SECOND

Mrs. Domville's *villa at Richmond.* Mrs. Domville *and* George Round *discovered.*

Round. The reason of my "wicked return," ma'am, is simply the respect I owe you, and the respect I owe to my cousin, your too amiable daughter.

Mrs. Domville. Have you forgotten that I informed you six months ago how you could best express that respect?

Round. By keeping out of your sight—by permitting you to forget my existence and encouraging you to hope I had forgotten yours? I obeyed your command, ma'am; I immediately joined my ship. But my ship came back last week.

Mrs. Domville. It didn't come back to Richmond, I suppose. This house is not your port!

Round. I think, indeed, rather, it's a rough and unfriendly coast!

Mrs. Domville. Take care, then, what befalls you in attempting to land.

Round. What worse can befall me than what befell me six months ago? The life was knocked out of me then, and if I meet your eyes once more it's simply that the mere wreck of my old presumption has been washed ashore at your feet.

Mrs. Domville. I'll warrant you a wreck that will take some time to sink—though indeed you do seem to have parted, in the tempest, with your uniform.

ROUND. On calculation, ma'am. As you appear to despise my profession, or at least my want of advancement in it, I thought it good taste not to fly my poor colours.

MRS. DOMVILLE. The taste of your calculations is better than that of your tailor!

ROUND. A man's tailor doesn't matter, perhaps, when he hasn't come to conquer. I am no longer a suitor for your daughter's hand. But I have a right to remind you—and this, ma'am, has been my errand—that I never promised to forget the tie of blood, the fine freedom of kinship.

MRS. DOMVILLE. The fine freedom of exaggeration! You blow the trumpet too loud over the ridiculous honour of having been poor Mr. Brasier's nephew.

ROUND. Why is it more ridiculous for *me* to have been his nephew than for *her* to have been his daughter?

MRS. DOMVILLE. (*After a moment.*) It ain't!

ROUND. I've come to tell you that I engage to make the best of your conditions.

MRS. DOMVILLE. "Conditions," my dear creature? We offered you none whatever. You were condemned without appeal.

ROUND. Say then that I accept even that. A man is suffered to see his family before he's hanged!

MRS. DOMVILLE. That plea doesn't hold, sir, for my daughter has ceased to belong to your family!

ROUND. (*Blank.*) Pray, then, to what family does she belong?

MRS. DOMVILLE. To mine.

ROUND. Yours?

MRS. DOMVILLE. The ancient house of Domville —of whose history, and whose fidelity to the old persuasion, you needn't affect a barbarous ignorance. My daughter's about to enter it, as her mother—less worthy!—did ten years ago. She's to marry Mr. Domville of Gaye.

ROUND. Almighty Powers!

MRS. DOMVILLE. Kinsman for kinsman, he's a much finer figure—

ROUND. Than a paltry lieutenant in the King's Navy? For you, I can understand it. But for *her?*—has submission been so easy?

MRS. DOMVILLE. The poor child has submitted to *him!* She's in love, with the most brilliant of men —the talk of the town, the wonder of the day! She's as gay as a lark and as proud as a queen.

ROUND. I shall believe that when I have it from *her!*

(*Enter* LORD DEVENISH.)

LORD DEVENISH. By all that's undesired, sir—You!

ROUND. With her hand so splendidly bestowed, at any rate, there can be no longer any hindrance to my seeing her.

LORD DEVENISH. Surely in so changed a case, dear sir, there can no longer be any reason for it!

ROUND. You talk of reasons, my lord, only to remind me that I've been long in discovering that of the authority you appear to enjoy in the private concerns of this house!

MRS. DOMVILLE. Everyone knows his dear lordship is our oldest friend—and our most affable!

ROUND. His affability I'm scarce in a position to enjoy. I'm willing however to beg that you appeal to it to grant me permission to take leave of Miss Brasier face to face.

LORD DEVENISH. Egad, sir, if *my* voice on that matter were sought, I wouldn't give you even a minute to take leave of Mrs. Domville!

MRS. DOMVILLE. (*Gracious.*) *After* the important event, you can come as often as you like!

ROUND. The important event takes place—?

MRS. DOMVILLE. (*After a moment's hesitation.*)

We had given it out for Saturday; but we anticipate.

LORD DEVENISH. (*Emphatically.*) We anticipate.
The wedding's *to-night.*

ROUND. (*Aghast.*) To-night?

LORD DEVENISH. And my chaplain ties the knot!

ROUND. (*After an instant, concentrated.*) *Out*
on your knot! *Curse* your chaplain! (*Exit.*)

LORD DEVENISH. Curse the beggar's intrusion! Is
everything quite in hand?

MRS. DOMVILLE. What does it matter if she
doesn't see him?

LORD DEVENISH. Who can say what Mary sees?
But everything's quite in hand!

MRS. DOMVILLE. The wedding-gown hasn't come
home!

LORD DEVENISH. The bride's? It *will* come! Yours,
dear Madam, is at any rate in the house!

MRS. DOMVILLE. You don't remind me, I suppose,
that I've two old ones on the shelf. The third takes
longer to make!

LORD DEVENISH. Do you presume to convey to me
that you cry off our bargain?

MRS. DOMVILLE. You talk as if we were a pair of
hucksters in the market!

LORD DEVENISH. Fie on the comparison! Sover-
eign, treaty-making powers! Need I remind you of
the *terms* of our treaty? The day after your daughter, pursuant to my explicit undertaking, becomes
Mrs. Domville of Gaye, Mrs. Domville of Richmond, to crown the happy enterprise, becomes
Viscountess Devenish.

MRS. DOMVILLE. You make a great flourish of it,
but you've your engagement still to perform!

LORD DEVENISH. Ain't I performing, Madam,
every hour? Didn't I perform, just now, to that
rascal sailor?

MRS. DOMVILLE. That rascal sailor has given me

the fidgets! (*As he goes up.*) What are you going to do?

LORD DEVENISH. To say a word to Mary.

MRS. DOMVILLE. And what is that word to be?

LORD DEVENISH. Not, Madam, what I understand you fear: the voice of *nature*—in a tell-tale sigh. I stifle the voice of nature—for *you!*

MRS. DOMVILLE. Not for *me*. For *her;* and as a penance for all your falsity!

LORD DEVENISH. That I was ever false, Madam, was a pleasant fable of your own—to accompany the stern moral of your second marriage.

MRS. DOMVILLE. I would have married you out of hand when my compunction was fresh; but by the time I was free—

LORD DEVENISH. It had lost its early bloom? Fie upon compunction! Marry me for bravery! And suffer me to proceed. I must satisfy myself again—

MRS. DOMVILLE. That he has really brought her round? Pray if he sensibly hadn't, how could he be so at ease?

LORD DEVENISH. (*Laughing.*) He's mighty fond of "ease"! The fellow's a born man of pleasure.

MRS. DOMVILLE. It's not all such gentry that confer as much of it as they take!

LORD DEVENISH. He only desires to be agreeable to *you,* Madam.

MRS. DOMVILLE. He succeeded from the moment he looked at me.

LORD DEVENISH. That's sufficiently denoted every time you look at *him!* (*Bantering.*) I don't mean to hint that poor Mary has her *mother's* inclination—!

MRS. DOMVILLE. Her mother, my lord, if she were asked, would marry the dear creature on the spot. As it is, she can only bustle about to adorn a younger bride!

LORD DEVENISH. You'll go for the gown yourself?

MRS. DOMVILLE. In the biggest coach in my stables! I want to make everything sure!

LORD DEVENISH. Everything *is* sure! *(Seeing* GUY.) And surest of all, Mr. Domville! It's a gage of his trust to *look* at him!

*(Enter* GUY DOMVILLE.)

GUY. I've been at your lodgings, my lord, to pay you my punctual duty; feeling that I owed you on so great a day an early visit and a close embrace.

LORD DEVENISH. It has been to render you a like attention that I have just presented myself here.

MRS. DOMVILLE. I admire the way you quit your beds to do each other honour; above all when I think of the hour, last night, at which you must have got into them!

GUY. It was an hour, Madam, I admit, that left us no choice of conclusions. The bright star that commands my attendance had long since sunk to obscurity; that luminary, indeed, to find a single fault with it, shines all too fitfully and sets all too soon! When Miss Brasier vanished we went for comfort to my Lady Mohun—but her ladyship's comfort proved singularly cold.—She engaged us deeply at cards.

MRS. DOMVILLE. Surely there's a fine warmth in cards!

GUY. Only in the warm side of them! I lost, on the spot, to her ladyship almost the clothes that covered me!

LORD DEVENISH. Guy always loses to the ladies!

GUY. I oughtn't in modesty, I suppose, to lose my *garments!* But it's done advisedly, my lord, since by the common saying, that kind of ill-fortune makes another kind of good.

LORD DEVENISH. Good fortune in love. Hark to the fellow!

GUY. Perhaps on your example I ought to aim at

both kinds; but what's a man to do at ombre when a lady *corrects* the luck?

LORD DEVENISH. This lady would say you're to take no notice!

MRS. DOMVILLE. What on earth does his lordship mean?

GUY. I won't pretend not to know! I think I always know, now, what his lordship means.

MRS. DOMVILLE. Sometimes it's a doubtful safety.

GUY. (*Laughing.*) Oh, I've had a lifetime of safety, Madam!

LORD DEVENISH. (*Laughing.*) The wretch quite dotes on his danger!

MRS. DOMVILLE. It's such a dear *good* wretch—it needn't fear communications!

GUY. I don't know how good it is, cousin, but I'm learning every day how ignorant.

MRS. DOMVILLE. Your ignorance, love, was a mighty pretty thing!

GUY. It goes down like an ebbing tide! I pick up fresh feelings as you gather pink shells; and when I hold these shells to my ear I find in each the mysterious murmur of the world!

MRS. DOMVILLE. You've a trick of fine speeches that make us women refuse you nothing.

GUY. You women, Madam, are even kinder than I always supposed you. You gave me confidence, you know, and upon my soul, I delight in confidence. I don't know how much I inspire, but I revel in all I feel. On such a day as this, it's universal. It doesn't stop even at my tailor!

LORD DEVENISH. You may trust your tailor when he's *my* tailor!

GUY. Egad, my lord, you've ordered my very garters!

LORD DEVENISH. With an eye to your interesting air! We shall see you in white and gold.

MRS. DOMVILLE. You can see he likes a fine coat!

GUY. I think, Madam, I like a fine anything. I can carry, at any rate, what you put on my back —and I think I can carry my happiness! Let it keep coming—and let me keep trying it! As I said to Mary anon, I enjoy my very gratitude. I meant, Madam, to *you*.

MRS. DOMVILLE. I hope you don't *always* talk to her of *me!*

GUY. When I want to please her most of all.

LORD DEVENISH. Didn't I promise you'd fall into the way of it? Didn't I tell you at Porches that you didn't do justice to your parts?

GUY. You told me at Porches some truths, my lord; and as regards the aptitudes you're so good as to praise, I'm almost frightened—

LORD DEVENISH.⎫
MRS. DOMVILLE.⎭ (*Together.*) Frightened?

GUY. At the way your prophecy's fulfilled. You told me I should find knowledge sweet—and life sweeter—

LORD DEVENISH. And love sweetest of all.

GUY. I had a shrewd notion of that!

LORD DEVENISH. The rascal had tried his hand!

MRS. DOMVILLE. Of course he had turned heads ere now.

LORD DEVENISH. He sees how he has turned all ours!

GUY. It was not to turn heads I came, Madam, but to do my duty to my line.

MRS. DOMVILLE. And to help me, dear Guy, to do mine.

GUY. I think, if I may say so, that you make too much of yours.

MRS. DOMVILLE. (*Grave, sincere.*) You were not at Mr. Domville's deathbed.

LORD DEVENISH. (*As if with the privilege of having assisted at a most edifying scene.*) I *was*, my dear Guy!

MRS. DOMVILLE. And you never knew my boy.

LORD DEVENISH. You're taking the boy's place, you know.

GUY. Peace then to these guardian spirits.

LORD DEVENISH. Precisely. And before we sacrifice to them—

MRS. DOMVILLE. I *must* put my hand on the bride's petticoat. (*To* GUY.) Did she go to her room?

GUY. My only complaint of her is that she's there too much.

MRS. DOMVILLE. I'll send her back to you.

LORD DEVENISH. I'll instruct him that he's to keep her.

MRS. DOMVILLE (*To* GUY, *significant.*) Till her mother takes her. (*To* LORD DEVENISH.) Make sure of Father White. (*Exit.*)

LORD DEVENISH. She'd like to have it over this minute!

GUY. What in the world is she afraid of?—

LORD DEVENISH. Of your *other* love, my lad; your first!

GUY. (*Blank.*) My first?

LORD DEVENISH. I don't mean Mrs. Peverel!

GUY. (*Very grave.*) You couldn't, my lord—in decency.

LORD DEVENISH. Decency—bless us—looks quite another way; decency points to our Mother-Church! Mrs. Domville is jealous of *that* high mistress.

GUY. I don't know what I could do, that I haven't done, to set such jealousy at rest. There's scarcely a rule I haven't utterly abjured—there's scarcely a trust I haven't rigidly betrayed—there's scarcely a vow I haven't scrupulously broken! What *more* can a man do for conscience?

LORD DEVENISH. What a man does for conscience, Guy, comes back to him for joy!

GUY. Is that why *you're* so happy?

LORD DEVENISH. My happiness is the happiness of others.

GUY. Mine then ought to content you! Never once have I looked behind. I've taken what you've given me—I've gone where you led me—I've done what you've told me.

LORD DEVENISH. You've done it monstrous well!

GUY. And no one is the worse for me?

LORD DEVENISH. As a man of the world that's the only spot on your glory!

GUY. I must be sure that everyone is the *better* for me, for that makes me as right as the proof of a sum!

LORD DEVENISH. (*Smiling.*) You'll be precious sure to-morrow!

GUY. Then let to-morrow come, and many many to-morrows!

LORD DEVENISH. Egad, we're catching up with them! I shall find Father White at his devotions.

GUY. Then let him *leave* his devotions! Remind him that *I've* left mine!

LORD DEVENISH. (*Attenuating.*) It's not after all to call him to cards! When Miss Brasier comes to you, be so good as to engage her closely.

GUY. (*Surprised.*) Will she grudge me her company?

LORD DEVENISH. Only from agitation. *Dispel* her agitation! (*Exit* LORD DEVENISH.)

GUY. Dispel her agitation? (*Thinking, with emotion.*) Face to face with my fortune I feel much more my own. Truly I've travelled far from all that might have been, and to say the words I must say, I must forget the words I didn't! (*Re-enter* GEORGE ROUND. *Startled.*) Pardon my inattention, sir, I didn't hear you announced.

ROUND. I came, sir, to deliver this packet to Miss Brasier.

GUY. Oh, another wedding-gift?

ROUND. Another wedding-gift.

GUY. From the toyman? A pretty bauble?

ROUND. A gold ring, sir—with a pearl.

GUY. (*Laughing.*) Only *one*? Pearls should come in dozens! But if you'll leave your packet with me, I'll take care Miss Brasier receives it.

ROUND. My errand, sir—my errand—

GUY. (*As he stands embarrassed.*) Was to place it in Miss Brasier's hand?

ROUND. To make sure it reaches her straight.

GUY. It shall reach her on this spot. She's coming to me. (*Then smiling as* ROUND *starts slightly.*) Quite lawfully, sir! I'm the bridegroom.

ROUND. (*After another hesitation.*) Then you can give it.

GUY. Is there anything to say with it?

ROUND. Only that I'll come back to see if it pleases. (*Exit.*)

GUY. To see if it pleases? For a tradesman, the fellow's blunt! (*Enter* MARY BRASIER.) You've just missed the toyman. He brought you a ring—with a pearl. (*Then as she appears blank and startled.*) Won't you look at it?

MARY. Give it to me.

GUY. From whom does it come?

MARY. (*With the box, in suppressed agitation.*) From no one. Where is the person who brought it?

GUY. He'll barely have reached the gate. Shall I call him?

MARY. (*Uneasy, prompt.*) No, no.

GUY. He's coming back to see if it pleases.

MARY. (*Troubled, but turning the matter off.*) It serves its purpose.

GUY. (*Laughing.*) Why, you've not even *tried* it!

MARY. It's a trifle—it's nothing! My mother told me to come to you.

GUY. (*Smiling.*) Your mother doesn't trust me!

MARY. I think she's wrong!

GUY. Do *you*, Mary? *Your* trust will be enough for me.

MARY. You're extraordinarily good to me.

GUY. How can I be good enough, when I think of all you're giving me?

MARY. (*With feeling.*) You ought to have more —than *I* can ever give!

GUY. More than beauty? More than virtue? More than fortune? More than your rising before me and letting me look into your eyes? I came here stammering and stumbling; but when I saw *you* it was as if I had caught the tune of my song!

MARY. Everything had been thoroughly arranged for you.

GUY. As things are arranged in the fairytales— only, you know, vastly better! The enchanted castle and the lovely princess, but never a giant nor a dragon.

MARY. (*Grave.*) The lovely princess seemed to *expect* the adventurous prince?

GUY. With all the charity in life! It was as if she too had been touched by the wizard.

MARY. She *had* been touched by the wizard!

GUY. (*With tender significance.*) The wizard whose name—?

MARY. (*Prompt.*) We mustn't *speak* it!

GUY. Because they never do, in fairytales, and our romance must conform to the rules. May our rules *all* be as easy! You leave me again?—You won't stay?

MARY. Yes, if I may make a condition. That of your telling me who brought the ring.

GUY. (*As if he had quite forgotten the incident.*) The ring?—from the toyman? Why, a young man with a brown face.

MARY. What sort of a manner?

GUY. No manner at all! You *know* him?

MARY. (*Embarrassed.*) I had better speak to him.

GUY. You easily can—he's coming back.

MARY. But *when,* did he say?

(*Re-enter* GEORGE ROUND.)

GUY. Here he is!

MARY. (*Greatly discomposed, but dissimulating; to* GUY.) Will you allow me five minutes with this gentleman?

GUY. (*Surprised.*) This gentleman?

ROUND. George Porter Round, at your particular service, sir.

MARY. I've something important to say to him.

GUY. (*Vague.*) Alone?

MARY. (*Finding a pretext.*) It's about *you!* And the ring.

GUY. (*Amused.*) Is it *my* finger it's to fit? Talk it over, then and send it back if it's not my quality! (*Exit.*)

MARY. (*With emotion.*) You've come *back!*

ROUND. I sent you back your early pledge as a sign.

MARY. I *have* it. I must give you back yours— that you so trustingly changed for it.

ROUND. Then the hideous story's true—and that's Mr. Domville?

MARY. You know then—you've been told?

ROUND. I was here an hour ago—straight from my ship.

MARY. You saw my mother?

ROUND. And your mother's— (*Catching himself up.*) The Lord Devenish.

MARY. They consented to your return?

ROUND. They opposed it—with all disparagement. But I've come back in spite of everything— for one glimpse of you!

MARY. They've hurried this business from the fear of you.

ROUND. Yet they must have little to fear of *you*—from your conduct!

MARY. Forgive me a little—*you* don't know!

ROUND. It's *I* who do know, Madam—and I think it's you who don't. They drove me off, and I went—in the state you may think. Then I got back my reason, and it came to me that I wanted you to know—to know that *I* know, and something, on my soul, of what I feel! I went to the goldsmith's in the town, and wrenching off that little ring of yours that I've worn so long, made him clap it into a new case. I thought some accident might protect me—that I might pass it in to you as coming from a shop. As fortune does sometimes favour the desperate, I succeeded. The coast was clear and I found myself face to face with *him!*

MARY. But this second time?

ROUND. The porter demurred, but passed me—for I asked for Mr. Domville. Mr. Domville had done me the honour—he still does it, happily—to mistake me for a peddler! But he had taken charge of my token.

MARY. The token of your inevitable scorn!

ROUND. When we parted, I could never have believed it!

MARY. We submitted, didn't we?—We consented to wait.

ROUND. In consenting I cursed your fortune, which made impatience look mercenary. If you had been poor, I would have consented to nothing!

MARY. My fortune is still the same. But some other things are different. The appeal to me pressed hard. And on my life it presses!

ROUND. Do you mean he makes such pretty love?

MARY. I'm speaking of my Lord Devenish. He's the oldest friend we have—he has ever studied to please me.

ROUND. I think *I've* studied harder! I don't know
what poison has worked in you, but I can't look on
you again without feeling that you're the thing in
the world I most desire! By the blessing of heaven
we're alone an instant, and all my life is yours!
Break with this monstrous betrayal, and commit
yourself to my guard. Escape while we *can* escape! I
came by the river, and my boat's at the garden-
foot.*

MARY. In a minute he'd miss me—he'd intercept
us; a public dispute? Not that. (*Then in deep dis-
tress.*) And there are contentions too ugly!

ROUND. But your mother's not here.

MARY. It would reach her. She's only at the milliner's.

ROUND. And your mother's friend?

MARY. His lordship? He's mustering the company.

ROUND. Then deal with this gentleman as we *can*.
Overreach him!

MARY. (*Vague.*) Deceive him?

ROUND. He *is* deceived—make it better. Break it
to him that I'm your cousin and that your mother
has put an affront on me. Bring us acquainted, and,
egad, we'll drink together!

MARY. (*Blank.*) Drink?

ROUND. (*Going up to table.*) Permit me to prove
the liquor. (*Pours out a glass and drinks.*) Faith,
it'll do. I can carry more than he.

MARY. (*Blank.*) But what do you purpose?

ROUND. To draw him on to it, and lay him on the
floor.

---

* The drinking scene which ensues here was deleted by
Henry James from the play after the first performance. The
reader desiring to obtain an idea of the emended version
must skip from Round's speech here to page 171 where, at
the point indicated below, the play continued with Round
still speaking: "It's *me, love,* you'll marry to-night!"

(*Re-enter* GUY.)

MARY. Hush!

GUY. (*Surprised and amused before* ROUND *has time to set down his glass*.) Ah, the wine-cup already flows.

ROUND. For a very thirsty messenger!

GUY. (*Smiling and addressing* MARY.) The messenger's perquisite? Then you've settled the great question?

ROUND. We've agreed on what's to be done. Shall I disclose it, Madam?

MARY. Disclose it.

(*Exit* MARY *upstairs*.)

ROUND. (*Promptly moving back to table*.) I was faintish a moment since—I've had a long walk in the sun.

GUY. Then help yourself, man. (*Then as* ROUND *appears shy about handling the wine*.) You'd rather I should help you?

ROUND. (*While* GUY *pours it for him*.) You're most obliging, but I'd fain take it *with* you, sir.

GUY. (*Surprised*.) "With" me? (*Laughing. Accommodating*.) It's the wedding feast begun!

ROUND. (*With his full glass*.) For the poor folk that are not bidden!

GUY. None shall be poor to-day! You're drinking a royal wine.

ROUND. I shall feel more worthy of it if I *share* it with you.

GUY. (*More surprised, but still amused; humouring him*.) To the complete restoration of your comfort!

ROUND. (*As if still unwell*.) To the speedy establishment of yours! (*Waits for* GUY *to drink; then on* GUY's *smiling and waiting, drains his glass*.) I think another would *right* me!

GUY. (*Offering his own untouched glass*.) Then take this!

ROUND. (*Reluctant.*) Yours?—*You* take it! (GUY *drinks and fills again for* ROUND, *and then again, on* ROUND *insisting, for himself; and, glass in hand, they look at each other, till* ROUND *breaks out suddenly as if the wine has begun to go to his head.*) I *ain't* the toyman!

GUY. (*Amazed.*) For whom I mistook you?

ROUND. (*Trying it on further.*) No, I ain't a peddler! (*Familiar, sociable.*) 'Pon my soul I ain't a peddler.

GUY. (*Blank, but still amused.*) Then who the devil *are* you?

ROUND. George Porter Round—lieutenant in the King's Navy! Near relation—in fact *poor* relation! —to that virtuous lady!

GUY. (*So mystified that he doesn't believe it.*) Who yet didn't introduce you—to the man she's about to marry?

ROUND. Her mother's liquor, you see, has done that.

GUY. (*Still sceptical and increasingly astonished.*) It shouldn't be left to the liquor, sir—and to the accident of a glass too much!

ROUND. Whose is the glass too much? Not yours, sir—no glass at all! Not mine, sir—glass too little! Leave, on the contrary, *everything* to the liquor! (*With the appearance of growing more fuddled.*) The liquor good enough for anything. The liquor as good as the young lady and much better than the old!

GUY. (*As if the incident is beginning to strike him as more serious.*) Pray in what relation do you stand—?

ROUND. Relation of worm in the dust! I mean to the old one!

GUY. (*With a nervous laugh.*) *I* mean to the young one!

ROUND. Relation of first cousin—nephew of poor

Mr. Brasier. Remember poor Mr. Brasier?

GUY. (*After a moment, but still smiling.*) I neither remember Mr. Brasier, sir, nor quite understand Mr. Brasier's nephew!

ROUND. Take me down that and you *will!* (*Then as* GUY, *with growing bewilderment and still glass in hand, hesitates to drink.*) Won't drink, either, with a poor relation?

GUY. (*As if this note touches him.*) I will indeed, if it will give you pleasure. (*Drains his glass.*)

ROUND. Nothing will give me so much!—Fill it again!

GUY. (*Again nervously laughing.*) I'm afraid I haven't quite your head!

ROUND. (*Imitating complete intoxication.*) *I've* no head—worm in the dust! Is a man of your rank afraid?

GUY. Not of you, sir!

ROUND. Then fill it again. (*Insistent, persuasive.*) You should be free on your wedding day.

GUY. (*After a moment.*) I'll be free! (*Drains another glass.*)

ROUND. (*Confidentially.*) The old lady *loves* me —not a bit! That's why the young lady—never mentions me at all! Quite ashamed of me too!— Keep it up!

GUY. (*After he has courteously complied by drinking a little.*) I should have been glad to hear of you sooner.

ROUND. Never too late to mend! But she has a feeling heart; bless it, I say.

GUY. Miss Brasier? Bless it by all means.

ROUND. I thank you for that, you know. I particularly thank you.

GUY. Why the devil so particularly?

ROUND. Oh, you'll see, sir, if you ain't proud. (*Motioning him to keep it up.*) Come, don't be proud. You are when you don't meet me. (*Going up to table for another decanter.*)

GUY. What trap is he baiting? I'll be caught.

ROUND. (*Foolishly ingratiating.*) Meet me *once* in your life! \*

GUY. (*After a moment, with his suspicion of* ROUND's *design now fairly kindled.*) I'll *meet* you! I know who you are, sir.

---

\* The text of *Guy Domville* reveals clearly, as indicated above, that Henry James expunged the drinking scene from the play after the ill-fated first night. But a scrap of dialogue found among his papers shows that he would have liked to retain at least part of the scene, emending it only to render it more plausible. The dialogue was intended to be inserted as follows, after Round says "Meet me *once* in your life!"

GUY. (*As before.*) I'll meet you!

           (*Re-enter* MARY.)

I was about to *meet* him, Madam.

MARY. (*Troubled.*) I came back to save you—

ROUND. (*Assured, disappointed.*) Save him from *what?* He ain't proud!

GUY. (*To* MARY.) *He* has cured me, I think, of pride!

MARY. May I speak to him again?

GUY. Is it very necessary?

MARY. It's a word or two more—I *must* say it.

GUY. You may say it on a condition: that he give me his hand. Will you give it to me, sir?

MARY. (*As* ROUND *hangs back.*) Won't you give him your hand? Do it for me!

GUY. (*Checking her; very gravely.*) Enough, Madam. I'm answered.

MARY. (*Uneasy, unhappy.*) You should be answered *better!*

GUY. (*At the door.*) It will serve!

           (*Exit* GUY.)

ROUND. (*Impatient, semi-reproachful.*) In a moment I should have *had* him; he thinks I'm tipsy—he was coming on!

MARY. He was *not* coming on—and I couldn't allow it. He saw you were acting—he knows we have a secret!

ROUND. (*Astounded.*) Then why does he leave us with it?

MARY. Because he thinks I've taken part—! It's a crime to practise on him: he's too *good!*

At this point James intended the play to proceed, as in the case of the previous deletion, from the speech on page 171 "It's *me, love,* you'll marry to-night!"

ROUND. (*Coming down with decanter and filling for* GUY *who with a changed manner, frankly welcomes it.*) I've filled to your wedding day.

GUY. You've filled, my dear fellow, but I'll be hanged if you've drunk!—Let me set you the example! (*Drinks deep.*)

ROUND. (*Who still doesn't drink.*) What do you think of the wine?

GUY. No judgment till the fifth glass!—Left your ship to come and see us?

ROUND. I left it last week. We had been three months out.

GUY. Three months out (*vaguely computing*) is just what *I've* been out! Devil of a time to be at the mercy of the waves!

ROUND. (*Laughing.*) That's the opinion of a judge who has not been much at sea!

GUY. Why, I'm at sea this blessed moment—never more at sea in all my life! A pack of things may happen in the course of three months—you may make a devil of a run. *I've* made a devil of a run—been off and round the world! Ever been round the world, in a cockle-shell like mine? (*Then laughing as* ROUND *laughs.*) I've trusted my life to a craft—as odd as any afloat. I think it's beginning to blow—do you suppose my boat'll hold? I put out, like you, this summer—but I haven't come into port.

ROUND. (*Hilarious.*) If you haven't come into port, I'll be bound you've come into burgundy. Take care how you sail your ship!

GUY. Got my orders, you know, for a voyage—a voyage of—What-do-you-call-it? You know what I mean to convey—'spedishun o' 'scovery!

ROUND. (*Looking round the place.*) Blest if you haven't made, then, a monstrous fine coast!

GUY. Mons'ous fine coast, Mons'ous fine house.

Mons'ous fine wine. Mons'ous fine women. 'Spedishun o' 'scovery!

ROUND. (*Allowing himself to become soberer as*
GUY *appears more tipsy.*) I, on my side, have discovered a monstrous fine gentleman in monstrous
fine clothes!

GUY. Mons'ous fine clo'se! Clo'se and clo'se and
clo'se! *See* me to-night in my clo'se—dance to-night
at my what-do-you-call-it? (*Then as if apprehending
refusal.*) *Don't* dance in the King's Navy?—*Teach*
you, egad, to dance! (*More and more falsely fuddled.*) Fifth glass. Now for judgment! Judgment
good. (*Hilariously.*) Keep it up, toyman!

ROUND. The moral of my visit, you know, is that
I'm positively *not* a toyman!

GUY. Then why the missch'f come with little
box?

ROUND. The little box was only a little present
for the bride.

GUY. It wasn't for the bridegroom?

ROUND. (*Filling for him in the exhilaration of
the success of his own plan.*) The best offering for
the bridegroom, sir, is another bumper of wine!

GUY. (*Stupidly submitting.*) Sixth glass—judgment bad.—Why do you drink so much? (*Raising
his glass.*) To the health of old friends! (*Holding
out his hand in foolish amity.*) No such comfort in
trouble as the clasp of the *hand* of old friends.
(*Then as* ROUND, *with a stiff, instinctive scruple,
holds off from accepting his hand.*) We *ain't* old
friends? We ain't poor relations? Come I've drunk
enough to cure me o' pride!

ROUND. Then I'll even drink to my cruel cousin!

GUY. (*With his glass raised.*) To the good health
of Mrs. Domville?

ROUND. Ah, never—I mean of the girl!

GUY. (*Abruptly, with capricious tipsy irritation.*)

Thank you to girl me no "girls"—on such a day as this!

(*Enter* MARY.)

ROUND. (*Good humoured.*) I mean of the sweet young lady!

GUY. (*As abruptly mollified.*) *I* mean of the sweet young lady. To the health of the sweet young lady. Here she *comes,* the sweet young lady! Your own relation, one of these days *my* relation, *our* relation. Keep it up!

ROUND. Now you see him, Madam, for what he is.

GUY. Eighth glass. Judgment gone!

ROUND. So indecently drunk that his very grossness belies his professions.

GUY. I'll be free, free on my wedding day.

ROUND. Fly with me now.

MARY. I cannot!

ROUND. You do love him, then?

MARY. No, no!

GUY. 'Spedishun of discovery! (*Exit* GUY.)

ROUND. It's *me, love,* you'll marry tonight! *

MARY. (*Painfully agitated and divided.*) How *can* I till I've seen my lord again? He put it to me so dreadfully on Sunday that I could save his life. My mother has promised to marry him! Overwhelmed with debt and difficulty, he has *that* one issue. But she becomes his wife only if *I* become Mr. Domville's!

ROUND. You spoke to me often of your mother's great taste for the Domvilles—but you never spoke to me of yours!

MARY. I *have* none. But I felt a private obligation to listen to my lord. I don't know *what* it was touched my heart when he went down on his knees to me! I thought I might tell him I'd please him—

---

* Henry James picked up the dialogue at this point after the deletion of the drinking scene.

and yet escape with my honour. I believed Mr.
Domville would guess the truth in time—would set
me free. But now I must *face* my lord!

ROUND. Mr. Domville holds fast to your money!

MARY. Don't say that when he's so good to me!

ROUND. If he doesn't, he has only to know the
truth to give you up.

MARY. He can only know it if I tell him!

ROUND. Tell him, then—tell him *now*. If you
don't, your heart is *false* to me!

MARY. It's not false, but it's cruelly torn. Don't I
owe a *duty* to my lord—to repay him for the kindness of years?

ROUND. You owe him *no* duty that's a sacrifice;
you're the creature in the world of whom he's least
entitled to demand one! (*After a moment of indeci-
sion.*) I know to-day what I didn't know when we
parted—what it appears that everyone else knows,
and what I shouldn't have been fool enough to be
blind to if I hadn't tasted more of my ship's mess
than of the London tea-tables, that the man who is
ready to traffic in your innocence with Jews and
gamesters—

MARY. (*Crying out with dread.*) Ah, what are
you going to tell me?

ROUND. Will you leave this house with me?

MARY. Not till I learn the worst!

ROUND. The Lord Devenish, Madam—is your
father.

MARY. (*Horror-stricken.*) My father!

ROUND. (*Seeing* GUY.) Hush!

(*Re-enter* GUY, *as much changed from beginning of Act as between Acts First and
Second.*)

GUY. (*With excited sternness.*) Our time is precious. You're attached to this lady!

ROUND. I'm in the very act of begging her to

place herself under my honourable protection.

GUY. You're not in danger, Madam—if you're unhappy!

MARY. If you've been deceived, it's not I who first deceived you.

ROUND. Miss Brasier has been acting from the first under compulsion damnable!

MARY. (*To* ROUND.) Will you let *me* tell him?

ROUND. Ah, if you'll be quick!

MARY. (*To* GUY.) Will you guard him—will you preserve him?

GUY. You ask strange things of me! But I'll preserve him the more that I think I've not quite done with him. I'm at your service, sir, in any place.

MARY. (*To* ROUND.) *Leave* me with him!

GUY. Stay, sir—one word! You put on me just now a strange undertaking.

ROUND. And what undertaking had you first put on *me?*

GUY. That's exactly what we shall clear up.

MARY. (*Alarmed.*) My mother's coach—she's back!

ROUND. Do you wish me, sir, to *encounter* Mrs. Domville?

MARY. (*To* GUY.) Will you go and prevent her somehow from coming in?

GUY. (*With high emphasis.*) You love this gentleman?

MARY. I love him.

GUY. Then I'll do better. Will you pass in there?

ROUND. Shall I?

MARY. Mr. Domville's apartment.

GUY. Three fine rooms in a row, which I owe to the bounty of Mrs. Domville.

ROUND. Thank you, sir.

GUY. (*Closes door.*) Thank *you!* sir. (*Exit*

Round.)\* To what dire bewilderment am I exposed? I *see*—but I only *half* see; so I've kept you here—that in this dire bewilderment, and before we lose another moment, I may learn the truth.

Mary. Our engagement then has been a bargain between my mother and my lord! My mother was to marry him if you married *me*. My lord's quite ruined—he doesn't know where to turn.

Guy. And your mother's rich—and I was poor?

---

\* At this point James had a brief entrance for "Mrs. Domville with two milliner's girls" and the following scene, later eliminated, ensued:

Mrs. Domville. You dear inseparables! I understand your desire to be together; but I'm afraid that for a moment, (*to* Mary) long enough to pass on a petticoat, I must divide you. (*To* Guy.) You'll make it up later!—You *won't* give us ten minutes, to make sure of the set of a tucker?

Guy. As many minutes as you need, Madam. On such an occasion one can't make *too* sure!

Mrs. Domville. You haven't fallen out—at this time of day? Wait till you see her in white satin!

Mary. (*Distressed.*) Mother!

Guy. I should like indeed to see you in white satin!

Mrs. Domville. Then there ain't a moment to lose. May we have for five minutes the convenience of your bower? (*To the* Milliners.) Pass in there.

Guy. (*Protecting his door.*) Not in here! Forgive me if I seem ungracious; but my own preparations—

Mrs. Domville. Are going on with such taste? I hope indeed they're splendid!

Guy. With a splendour that will surprise you.

Mrs. Domville. Ah, then we won't spoil it! (*To* Mary.) Come quickly to your room.

Guy. Suffer me to speak to her first.

Mrs. Domville (*Disconcerted.*) After you've had the whole day?

Mary. It doesn't seem enough for what Mr. Domville has to say!

Mrs. Domville. The rascal has a tongue—even with *me!*

Guy. It's to settle a question of weight!

Mrs. Domville. Settle your question—but look at that shawl!

(*Exit* Mrs. Domville *with the* Milliners.)

MARY. You had the great name. She clings to that.

GUY. If his lordship caught me, he was to be paid?

MARY. Paid high! His lordship caught you!

GUY. Like a blind bat in a handkerchief. While I wondered at his love of the chase!

MARY. These things were dark to you—and they've but just grown clear to *me*.

GUY. Dark as deceit! Dark as dishonour! I believed too easily. I was tempted. You were offered to me—pressed upon me. And you were fair. You were given to me with a lie—a bribe! They declared you were free—were happy. Your submission itself misled me, for you suffered when you had only to speak.

MARY. I suffered, but I went on—I thought I was gaining time. Time, I mean, for you to see. But you were too dazzled.

GUY. I was dazzled by life!

MARY. You see what life is.

GUY. Some of it, yes. Why should you have feared to disappoint me, when I was nothing to you?

MARY. It wasn't you—it was my lord.

GUY. *He's* nothing to you.

MARY. He's my father.

GUY. (*Aghast.*) Your father?

MARY. I didn't know it then—I've known it but a moment. It makes strange things clear—the force of his appeal. That appeal was like a voice that cried to me to make a sacrifice of my affection. I tried, but it was more than I could do.

GUY. You paid for my folly, for my madness— you paid for the vices of others! And now we pay together!

MARY. (*With decision.*) We've paid enough— we're free!

GUY. *I* haven't paid—what I've cost you. (*Won-*

*dering, harking back.*) He's your *father?*

MARY. It *had* to come (*indicating* ROUND'S *refuge*) from *him!* It makes all the past confused.

GUY. And what does it make your mother?

MARY. *Forgive* my mother!

GUY. God pity us all! How can you forgive me for doing you so great a wrong?

MARY. You're already forgiven!

GUY. Ask *him* to forgive me. He had never harmed me. But I've hurt myself most; for I've been deluded with a delusion that was built upon an injury to others. It was to flaunt in it here that I was brought. But that's over. Good-bye.

MARY. Good-bye.

GUY. Yet if I go, how can I leave you to *them?*

MARY. Ah. Let me not *look* on them!

GUY. Shall I commit you rather to the man you love?

MARY. *Trust* him!

GUY. Then join him there. Here is a key that opens the door on the river.

MARY. He has a boat, thank God. (DEVENISH *is heard off centre calling,* "Guy—Guy.")

GUY. (*Coming down from the window.*) His lordship—be quick!

MARY. (*Apprehensive.*) But *you?*

GUY. Me? *I'll* look on him! (*With a laugh of bitterness.*) It serves me right!

MARY. (*Carrying his hand to her lips.*) Heaven do as much for *you!* (*Exit* MARY.)

(*Re-enter* LORD DEVENISH.)

LORD DEVENISH. My chaplain's robing—but you, dear boy, are *not!*

GUY. I've been here till this moment with Mary —engaging her closely, I promise you!

LORD DEVENISH. (*Laughing.*) I know the way you engage! You shall have guests enough—and noble ones. I put my hand on a score.

GUY. But none so noble as yourself, my lord!

LORD DEVENISH. I'm a neat figure, eh?

GUY. Scented like a duchess! Beams of light in clouds of fragrance!

LORD DEVENISH. Do I dazzle?—I love a fine odour! (*Holding out his gloves.*) Carry *that* to your nose!

GUY. (*Sniffing.*) My nose is regaled! (*Looking at the gloves.*) Something French, you prodigal? To the finger-tips! And every seam silver!

LORD DEVENISH. Straight from Paris. They set one off! Take 'em, my son.

GUY. (*Disconcerted.*) Take 'em?

LORD DEVENISH. Wear 'em to hand the bride. I've given you *nothing*.

GUY. You've given me too much, my lord!

LORD DEVENISH. Well, as you like! But you must be none the less a figure.

GUY. (*With a laugh.*) I've had a notion of my own for that!

LORD DEVENISH. Then quick, man; change!

GUY. I'll change! (*Exit.*)

LORD DEVENISH. He's half a monk still! (*Then laughing.*) But to-morrow—! (*Re-enter* MRS. DOMVILLE *followed by two* MILLINERS *carrying boxes.*) Ah, *you* at least are ready!

MRS. DOMVILLE. *Is Mary here?*

LORD DEVENISH. She was here till a moment since.

MRS. DOMVILLE. I've been to her room with these women.

LORD DEVENISH. Guy's dressing—we shall have a company!

MRS. DOMVILLE. We must first have a bride— and at least a footman!

LORD DEVENISH. The footmen are dressing too— making up white favours.

MRS. DOMVILLE. I bade them be brave—but not stone deaf!

LORD DEVENISH. The rascals are all at the barber's!

MRS. DOMVILLE. (*Calling out.*) Mary—Mary!—The hussy!

LORD DEVENISH. (*Calling.*) Mary! Mary!

MRS. DOMVILLE. Is she in there?

LORD DEVENISH. With Guy? Go and see.

(*Exit* MRS. DOMVILLE *to* GUY'S *apartment, where she is heard knocking and calling* "Cousin, cousin! Daughter, daughter!"

LORD DEVENISH, *alone. Enter a* FOOTMAN.)

LORD DEVENISH. You've come from above. Is Miss Mary there?

FOOTMAN. I've come across the water, my lord. Miss Brasier's left the house.

LORD DEVENISH. Left it for where?

FOOTMAN. I've taken a guinea, my lord, not to say.

LORD DEVENISH. Then take another, damn you, to do your duty.

FOOTMAN. By my duty then, my lord, she's off in a great boat, a gentleman close beside her and three watermen to pull.

LORD DEVENISH. The boat of a man of war. The ruffian, the serpent!

(*Enter* MRS. DOMVILLE.)

MRS. DOMVILLE. He's locked in. I'll be hanged if he'll answer.

LORD DEVENISH. This knave has sufficiently answered. The hussy's gone with the villain she was leagued with and who reached here in time.

MRS. DOMVILLE. And you saw it, and gave no alarm!

FOOTMAN. I only saw, Madam, what Mr. Domville himself saw. He waved his hat from the terrace.

LORD DEVENISH. Domville, the false wretch, has abetted them.

Mrs. Domville. Pursue them. Start the hue and cry!

Lord Devenish. Be off! The horse is stolen and it's all too late. From the moment they met we were dished. Let them go!

Mrs. Domville. (*Horrified.*) Go and be married?

Lord Devenish. Go and be damned. We still have Guy! He's as much of a Domville as ever! He can still have heirs.

Mrs. Domville. *He* can—but *I* can't!

Lord Devenish. Not of your body—but of your vows. *Mary* he never loved!

Mrs. Domville. More shame to him.

Lord Devenish. He's in love with Mrs. Peverel.

Mrs. Domville. (*Highly impatient.*) So are *you,* I believe, from the way you prate of her!

Lord Devenish. If I prate of her now, it's because our contract *stands.*

Mrs. Domville. How does it stand, when you've not performed your task?

Lord Devenish. My task, Madam, was not to hold Mary—it was to hold *Guy!* We *do* hold him, i'faith —through the blessed lady of Porches. If I don't demonstrate *that*—if I don't please you *still*—

Mrs. Domville. (*Taking the words out of his mouth.*) I may *then* turn you off? God knows I *will!*

Lord Devenish. And not, Madam, *before!* We can catch Mrs. Peverel—if we act in time: from this moment forth she's the only woman he'll look at. She'll retrieve our defeat.

Mrs. Domville. (*Breathless.*) Where are you going?

Lord Devenish. To Porches again—to see she doesn't marry her neighbour. (*Elated with his idea; confident.*) You'll marry *yours!* ( *Exit in hot haste.*)

Mrs. Domville. I believe I *shall*—before he has done with me! (*Then as she sees* Guy.) Mercy on us! (*Re-enter* Guy Domville *in plain array.*) What on earth, sir, have you done?

GUY. I think, Madam, I've done justice. I've seen them on their way.

MRS. DOMVILLE. Their way's a fine one!

GUY. It seems to me finer than mine has been. It seems to me finer even than yours!

MRS. DOMVILLE. (*Dismayed.*) Mine?

GUY. Yours.

MRS. DOMVILLE. (*Conscious, faltering.*) Does she —know?

GUY. She knows. She made *me* know. I helped her. Farewell!

MRS. DOMVILLE. (*In anguish, with a supreme appeal.*) Cousin!

GUY. (*Inexorable.*) Farewell!

MRS. DOMVILLE. Where are you going?

GUY. I'm going back! (*Exit.*)

# ACT THIRD

*The White Parlour at Porches. Door from the hall left; door to the bookroom right.* Mrs. Peverel *is seated by fire. Enter* Fanny *from the hall with a letter on a tray.*

Fanny. A letter, please, ma'am. (*Then as* Mrs. Peverel, *gazing at fire, doesn't answer.*) Please, ma'am, a *letter.*

Mrs. Peverel. (*Starting at last; eager.*) A letter? (*On looking at it, disappointed, uninterested, tosses it down unopened.*) Oh!

Fanny. And a whole shilling to pay, ma'am. (*Then, as* Mrs. Peverel *has dropped again into her reverie.*) He'll take nothing less than a shilling, ma'am.

Mrs. Peverel. (*Vaguely roused.*) A shilling?

Fanny. (*Picking the letter up.*) It's a deal to pay for a letter to lie on the floor!

Mrs. Peverel. Give him a shilling, child, and hold your tongue!

Fanny. But where am I to *find* the shilling, ma'am?—

Mrs. Peverel. With my money—where my money is.

Fanny. But *where's* your "money" in these dull days? (*Then perceiving a coin on the dresser.*) Here's a piece, ma'am.

Mrs. Peverel. Then give it to him!

Fanny. (*Dismayed.*) Give it *all?*

Mrs. Peverel. (*With an irritated, bored move-*

*ment, takes the coin from her; then without looking at it.*) Here's your money, man. Go!

FANNY. (*Aghast.*) Why, it was half a crown!

MRS. PEVEREL. I didn't heed!

FANNY. There are few things you *do* "heed," ma'am, just now!

MRS. PEVEREL. There's one thing I *must*! (*Indicating a book lying on a cabinet.*) Is that book Latin?

FANNY. Laws, ma'am, how should *I* know? (*Giving the book as if almost awestruck.*) Are you taking to "Latin," ma'am?

MRS. PEVEREL. For my son's lesson. Please tell him to come in and have it.

FANNY. He won't come in for *my* telling, ma'am.

MRS. PEVEREL. (*Flinging the book down disheartenedly.*) And he won't come in for mine!

FANNY. He'd only come in for a gentleman, I think.

MRS. PEVEREL. (*Musing.*) He must feel a stronger hand!

FANNY. Such another as Mr. Domville's!

MRS. PEVEREL. There *isn't* "such another"! Mr. Domville's was so strong—yet Mr. Domville's was so light.

FANNY. (*Glancing down complacently, while she gives it a turn, at the pocket of her apron.*) Mr. Domville was so *free*!

MRS. PEVEREL. (*With latent bitterness.*) Well, it's not "free" now!

FANNY. Do you mean he has lost money?

MRS. PEVEREL. (*Dryly.*) He has gained it. By his marriage.

FANNY. Mercy, ma'am, is he married?

MRS. PEVEREL. By this time—to-day.

FANNY. And he quite the same as a priest!

MRS. PEVEREL. He's *not* quite the same. He never *was*!

FANNY. Well, if he was here he'd pay for a fiddler—to make us all dance for his wedding!

MRS. PEVEREL. He'll never be here again!

FANNY. (*Sad, wistful.*) Nor any other gentleman at all? (*Prompt.*) I mean for the Latin!

MRS. PEVEREL. I'm looking for another. There should certainly *be* one.

FANNY. (*Diplomatic.*) I suppose they're precious hard to come by!

MRS. PEVEREL. (*With a weary sigh.*) Especially if one doesn't look!

FANNY. (*Circumspect, after a silence.*) Mr. Humber, ma'am—does *he* know Latin?

MRS. PEVEREL. I haven't the least idea what Mr. Humber knows!

FANNY. *I* have, ma'am—for *one* thing: he knows Mr. George is mighty fond of him.

MRS. PEVEREL. If Mr. George is mighty fond, Mr. George is mighty fickle! Mr. George shifts his affections!

FANNY. Mr. Humber don't—do he, ma'am?—Mr. Humber, ma'am, is constant.

MRS. PEVEREL. (*With a sudden flare of irritation and perversity.*) Then why hasn't he *been* here for weeks?

FANNY. (*At the window, startled.*) Law, ma'am, he *is* here now! He's at the door in his coach!

MRS. PEVEREL. (*More capriciously still, with decision.*) Then he mustn't get out!

FANNY. He *is* out—he's coming in.

MRS. PEVEREL. I won't see him. (*Dismissing* FANNY, *getting her off.*) Meet him—stop him—send him away! (*Exit* FANNY.) I *won't* see him! (*After an instant.*) I can't! (*After another instant.*) I oughtn't!

(*Re-enter* FANNY, *breathless.*)

FANNY. He's on the stairs—now!

MRS. PEVEREL. Then I must be tidy! (*Exit hastily to the bookroom.*)

(*Enter* FRANK HUMBER.)

FANNY. She's in the bookroom—she'll come.

FRANK. Thank you, Fanny. What's the good news at Porches?

FANNY. There's neither good nor bad at Porches, sir; but there's wonderful news at Richmond. Mr. Domville's married to-day! (*Exit to the hall.*)

FRANK. (*Immediately affected.*) To-day?—Will *that* help me? Nothing will help me! (*Re-enter* MRS. PEVEREL.) You must wonder at the motive of my visit.

MRS. PEVEREL. It was never my wish that you should never come back.

FRANK. It was once mine. It was at least my purpose.

MRS. PEVEREL. (*Kindly.*) I rejoice in your recovery from so desperate a mood.

FRANK. If it was a mood, Madam, it was a mood that has remained. The purpose I speak of has grown.

MRS. PEVEREL. Then your visit is certainly odd!

FRANK. It's worse than "odd"—it's abject! But I've ceased to pretend to make a figure!

MRS. PEVEREL. You place me in the painful position of scarce being able to show you that I'm sorry to see you so altered.

FRANK. I doubt not you're sorry, Madam—and there can be nought but sorrow between us. I'm leaving the country.

MRS. PEVEREL. (*Surprised.*) For where—for what?

FRANK. For the ends of the earth—and for everything!

MRS. PEVEREL. (*Anxious.*) For a long time?

FRANK. For ever!

MRS. PEVEREL. (*Astonished, compassionately remonstrant.*) But your estate? your home?

FRANK. What *use* have I for a "home"—a home empty and barren? We're neighbours, after all, till I go; so I come to take leave of you.

MRS. PEVEREL. You go to travel?

FRANK. I go to wander.

MRS. PEVEREL. And who goes *with* you?

FRANK. I go alone.

MRS. PEVEREL. Alone into strange lands—alone into exile?

FRANK. It's better than alone here: close to you, yet separate!

MRS. PEVEREL. It seems to me then it's *I* who ought to go!

FRANK. (*Startled, flickering up.*) If you do, I'll follow you!

MRS. PEVEREL. Then I'll *stay!* (*Sadly smiling.*) I'll not follow *you!*

FRANK. I wish you a long life—in all this tranquillity!

MRS. PEVEREL. I shall remember you well—I shall miss you much. I'm not a woman of many friends —I've not a life of many diversions. This country will seem an empty place.

FRANK. All the more that I can recall, without a reminder, the loss you lately suffered.

MRS. PEVEREL. As I can allude to it without a scruple. Mr. Domville's a support—withdrawn. Do you know what happens to-day?

FRANK. (*With a glance at the clock.*) It's over?

MRS. PEVEREL. It's over. I wish him all happiness and length of days!

FRANK. I wish him all peace and plenty! Plenty of children, I mean! A numerous and virtuous posterity!

MRS. PEVEREL. (*Abrupt, irrelevant.*) Is your beautiful house to be closed?

FRANK. It will always be open to *you*. It's full of my grandmother's books—old novels in ten volumes. If you lack diversions you can go and take down the "Grand Cyrus" * or eat pears† in the great garden.

MRS. PEVEREL. (*With a frank smile.*) Along with the child? Do you want to kill him? There are too many pears for him *here!*

FRANK. (*Beguiled, with a laugh.*) Is he perched even now in a tree?

MRS. PEVEREL. We'll go anon together and pull him out!—What strange land do you go to first?

FRANK. (*Impatiently.*) What does it matter, when they're all strange alike?

MRS. PEVEREL. (*With sudden feeling.*) Mr. Humber—forsake this wild plan! Don't give up your own lands and your own people—don't give up the sweet, safe things you love!

FRANK. (*With a newborn, unexpected tremor of hope and suspense.*) Don't give *you* up—is that what you mean?

MRS. PEVEREL. I mean— (*Faltering.*) I mean—!

(*Re-enter* FANNY.)

FANNY. (*Loudly announcing.*) My Lord Devenish!

(*Enter* LORD DEVENISH.)

LORD DEVENISH. I came in the hope of finding you alone, Madam.

MRS. PEVEREL. Mr. Humber is going to a great distance. He is here to bid me good-bye.

LORD DEVENISH. Well, if that affecting ceremony is over I should like the honour of half-an-hour's conversation with Mrs. Peverel.

FRANK. (*Disconcerted, resentful.*) That affecting ceremony is by no means "over"!

* *Artamène, ou le Grand Cyrus,* a French heroic romance by Madeleine de Scudéry (1607-1701) was published in ten volumes between the years 1649-53. The translation was very popular in England.

† James originally wrote "plums" then substituted "pears."

LORD DEVENISH. (*Unperturbed.*) May I none the less, in view of the extreme importance of time in the case, venture to ask Mrs. Peverel for an immediate interview?

MRS. PEVEREL. I've no doubt Mr. Humber will excuse me, since (*smiling at* FRANK) I'm sure his haste is less than yours!

FRANK. (*Significantly.*) My haste, thank God, is less than when I came, Madam!

LORD DEVENISH. That's good news if it refers to Mr. Humber's leaving the country.

MRS. PEVEREL. (*To* FRANK.) If you must go—

FRANK. (*In suspense.*) If I must go?

MRS. PEVEREL. (*Smiling.*) You can first pull Geordie out of the tree!

FRANK. (*Displeased, with decision.*) I'll get into it *with* him! (*Exit.*)

LORD DEVENISH. Mr. Domville, Madam, is *free!* His wonderful marriage is off!

MRS. PEVEREL. (*Astonished.*) And what has occurred to stay it?

LORD DEVENISH. Everything has occurred—and on top of everything my coming down here to tell you so. You may expect Mr. Domville in this place, and I judged it wise to prepare you for his return. To that good end I've got here first.

MRS. PEVEREL. (*Anxious.*) Does he follow anon?

LORD DEVENISH. Oh, not till he has turned round, I conceive—found his feet and recovered his fall from the height of his great match. In honest terms, Madam, he has been misused.

MRS. PEVEREL. (*Startled, with indignation.*) Jilted?—*Such* a man?

LORD DEVENISH. By practices most underhand! The young lady was clandestine!

MRS. PEVEREL. She must have been abominable!

LORD DEVENISH. (*Just visibly wincing.*) She was

beguiled, Madam, by a villain!—Mr. Domville has suffered much.

MRS. PEVEREL. I vow I pity him!

LORD DEVENISH. He knows that you *must!*

MRS. PEVEREL. And that's why he's coming? I shall indeed be kind to him!

LORD DEVENISH. Kind, Madam, but firm! Firm with his inclination.

MRS. PEVEREL. (*Struck, apprehensive.*) You mean he'll take up again—

LORD DEVENISH. The cruel profession he forsook? That's the fear that has brought me! Suffer him, Madam, *not* to! You'll find a way when you see him. You'll see a braver gentleman; greater by the greatness I've taught him!

MRS. PEVEREL. (*Much interested.*) He must have a different air!

LORD DEVENISH. Finer, Madam, and nobler! To stifle such an air in a *cassock*—

MRS. PEVEREL. Would be a grievous sin! But why, if he's only dejected, should he come to this dull place?

LORD DEVENISH. (*With great intended effect, as if having waited for just the right moment to make the revelation.*) "Why," Madam? Because he loves you! Because he worships you!

MRS. PEVEREL. (*Astounded, confounded.*) And yet was so ready to wed another woman?

LORD DEVENISH. Overborne by Mrs. Domville! He never *loved* Miss Brasier.

MRS. PEVEREL. (*Catching her breath; stupefied.*) Never loved her?

LORD DEVENISH. He feels the indignity, but not the loss; and he had never dreamed that with *you,* who had only known him as the tutor of your son and the nursling of the Church, there was the smallest human hope for him. The way to save him is to *give* it to him! *That,* Madam, is the truth I came to utter. Having satisfied my conscience, I retire. To pay another visit in the West. (*Invitingly, persuasively.*) I shall not be too far to hear from you.

MRS. PEVEREL. To hear, I judge you mean, from Mr. Domville.

LORD DEVENISH. I bow to your modesty! But Mr. Domville had better not know—

MRS. PEVEREL. Of your lordship's kind warning?

LORD DEVENISH. Don't advertise my kindness!

MRS. PEVEREL. Your presence will be the talk of the village.

LORD DEVENISH. The village is dumb—my carriage is a mile off.

MRS. PEVEREL. And you walk back to it?

LORD DEVENISH. (*Smiling, urbane, successful, with the movement of complacently swinging a cane.*) Across the quiet fields!

MRS. PEVEREL. But Mr. Humber has seen you.

LORD DEVENISH. Isn't Mr. Humber going?

MRS. PEVEREL. (*After an instant.*) I can't answer for it!

LORD DEVENISH. (*Smiling.*) I should have thought it the thing in the world you could *most* answer for! Ask him to hold his tongue!

MRS. PEVEREL. (*Embarrassed, considering.*) I'm scarce in a position to ask him a service.

LORD DEVENISH. (*As if struck by a new and intenser idea.*) Then send him to *me!*

(*Re-enter FANNY, carrying a tray of refreshments and wine, which she places on a table.*)

MRS. PEVEREL. I'll send him! (*To FANNY.*) What wine have you brought?

FANNY. The best, ma'am—and the other.

MRS. PEVEREL. (*Smiling at LORD DEVENISH.*) Don't give his lordship the "other"! (*Exit.*)

FANNY. (*Pouring out wine.*) Mr. Domville, my lord, used to like it!

LORD DEVENISH. (*After he has tasted the wine.*) Mr. Domville wouldn't like it now!

FANNY. I suppose there's much better in London.

LORD DEVENISH. (*Amused.*) There's nothing much better in London, my dear, than a pretty country lass!

FANNY. (*Curtseying low.*) Oh, my lord!

LORD DEVENISH. (*Quickly.*) Go away!

(*Re-enter* FRANK HUMBER. *Exit* FANNY.)

FRANK. Your lordship desires my company?

LORD DEVENISH. (*Pouring out a second glass.*) To have a glass with you. (*Then after a conscious pretence, on each side, of drinking.*) Mr. Domville's in love with this lady!

FRANK. (*Blank.*) In the very act of marrying another?

LORD DEVENISH. He's *not* in the act. The act's undone; through his coldness at the last. The young lady guessed it—the young lady broke!

FRANK. (*Amazed.*) And he took back his word?

LORD DEVENISH. (*Very ready.*) She took back hers! He retired in silence, conscious of his secret preference.

FRANK. (*After a moment; coldly, stiffly.*) The object of such a preference is surely *most* concerned—!

LORD DEVENISH. That object, sir, he has never addressed!—Do you conceive that Mrs. Peverel would *listen* to him?

FRANK. (*Dryly.*) I know nothing about it. How is it I can serve your lordship?

LORD DEVENISH. (*Consciously rebuffed, but still assured.*) By acting a noble part. It rests with *you* to rout Father Murray. (*With commanding authority.*) Mr. Domville must *marry*!

FRANK. (*Struck, sombre.*) Marry Mrs. Peverel?

LORD DEVENISH. Understand that he *may!*

FRANK. What *prevents* his understanding?

LORD DEVENISH. (*Very pointedly.*) If *you* know of nothing, sir, the question I wish to ask you is answered!

FRANK. (*Deeply troubled, thinking.*) He *loves* her—Guy?

LORD DEVENISH. Did you never scent it?

FRANK. Why, he spoke to her for *me,* when, never supposing, never *dreaming,* I pushed him to 't!

LORD DEVENISH. (*Decided.*) Then *that,* of course, prevents him!

FRANK. (*Still realizing, remembering.*) For *me*— poor wretch—when he loved her himself!

LORD DEVENISH. Mr. Domville was magnanimous!

FRANK. He was heroic! You call upon *me* to be so, my lord. There's only *one* way! Not to talk of absence, but to practise absence. If I'm gone, he'll know why!

LORD DEVENISH. I'll take care he knows why!
(*Re-enter* MRS. PEVEREL.)

MRS. PEVEREL. (*Breathless.*) Mr. Domville! His carriage has entered the gate.

FRANK. (*Strongly disconcerted.*) And I'm not off!

LORD DEVENISH. (*Deeply dismayed.*) And I still less! (*At left, hurriedly.*) I leave you, Madam.

MRS. PEVEREL. Not *that* way—you'll meet him!

FRANK. (*Putting out his hand to* MRS. PEVEREL.) Farewell!

MRS. PEVEREL. (*Keeping his hand.*) You won't wait to take leave of him?

LORD DEVENISH. (*Pressing.*) You should do *that,* Mr. Humber! (*Then while* FRANK *gives a gesture of pained resignation.*) How then am I to go?

MRS. PEVEREL. (*Anxious, at a loss.*) Some other way!

FRANK. (*Surprised.*) Your visit's private?

LORD DEVENISH. (*Angrily.*) Private!

FRANK. (*Amusedly.*) His step's on the stair! Here he comes!

MRS. PEVEREL. (*Quickly, at the door right.*) Pass in!

(*Exit* LORD DEVENISH *on tiptoe.*)

FRANK. The bookroom—with no way out?

MRS. PEVEREL. (*Ruefully.*) None at all! (*Then making the best of it.*) I'll free him!—Silence!

(*Enter* GUY DOMVILLE.)

GUY. (*After having looked hard an instant from* MRS. PEVEREL *to* FRANK.) Forgive the old trick in the old place—I've come up as I used to come up.

MRS. PEVEREL. And you're welcome as you used to be welcome!

GUY. The abruptness of my return deserves, I fear, less honour.

MRS. PEVEREL. It shall have all we can give it—and that of some instant preparation for your staying.

GUY. Madam, I didn't come to quarter myself—

MRS. PEVEREL. (*Ironic.*) Anywhere but on the baker?

GUY. I sent on my shay to the inn.

MRS. PEVEREL. It shall come back! (*Exit.*)

GUY. (*After precautions; in eager suspense.*) Has she accepted you?

FRANK. She has *not* accepted me!

GUY. Then, since I helped you, spoke for you, did everything I *could* for you, I tell you that she's dearer to me than *life*, that I'm not bound but free, and that I've come back again to tell her so!

FRANK. I know to what tune she's "dear" to you!

GUY. (*Astonished.*) You know it?

FRANK. Take care!

(*Re-enter* MRS. PEVEREL.)

MRS. PEVEREL. I've sent for your shay.

GUY. (*Gratefully resigned.*) Then I'm in your hands! (*Unsuspiciously, to* FRANK.) You're going?

FRANK. (*Impenetrable.*) I'm going!

GUY. But I shall see you again!

FRANK. You'll have to be alert! And only, too, if so soon again this lady will consent to part with you.

MRS. PEVEREL. (*Smiling.*) I think it will be found that the consent most necessary is Geordie's.

GUY. (*Completely genial.*) And how is that victim of the rudiments? Would he come and absolve his tormentor?

MRS. PEVEREL. In a moment, if he knew you were here.

GUY. Then won't you *let* him know?

FRANK. I'll acquaint him!

MRS. PEVEREL. (*Demurring, embarrassed.*) Not yet, please: say nothing! I've a reason for his not romping in!

GUY. (*To* FRANK.) I shall overtake you before you mount.

FRANK. (*In weary self-derision*). I shall only mount a cushion.

GUY. You drove?

FRANK. Like a helpless fat dowager—in an old yellow coach.

GUY. (*Concerned.*) Do you mean to say you're ill?

MRS. PEVEREL. (*Significantly.*) He knows the way to get better! (*The more gaily, to* FRANK.) Keep Geordie quiet! (FRANK, *at the door, looks at her fixedly a moment, as if on the point of saying something; then checking himself, exit rapidly.*) I needn't keep you here. We can talk as well—anywhere.

GUY. Shall we go into the garden?

MRS. PEVEREL. (*Demurring.*) We shall have the child!

GUY. (*Suggesting the bookroom.*) Then in there?

MRS. PEVEREL. No—it's encumbered!

GUY. (*Looking about him appreciatively, fondly.*) This old White Parlour has the friendly face to me! I've seen it, since we parted, in visions—I've missed it in grander places. Its panelled walls close me in—the tick of the clock seems to greet me. It's full of faint echoes and of lost things found again. We sat here o' winter nights.

MRS. PEVEREL. (*Coerced by his tone, wishing not to break the spell.*) Then we can sit here again!

GUY. I think it was for *that* I came back!

MRS. PEVEREL. (*Smiling.*) On the eve of your great marriage?

GUY. That eve has had no morrow!

MRS. PEVEREL. I fear you've been shamefully used!

GUY. Not by the person in whom I liked most to believe. That person was honest. But I think that, save at Porches, there are very few others who are.

MRS. PEVEREL. At Porches—if we're not much else —we're honest!

GUY. That's why my heart turned back to you and why my footsteps ran a race with it!—Do you remember how, at the last, we talked together of the world?

MRS. PEVEREL. You said all manner of ill of it!

GUY. I told you I'd come back to say more. I've seen it—and it doesn't answer!

MRS. PEVEREL. You must describe to me what you've seen.

GUY. Ah, much of it I wish to forget!

MRS. PEVEREL. What you must forget is that you've suffered.

GUY. What I must forget is that I've strayed!— from the happiness that was near to the happiness that was far!

MRS. PEVEREL. But the happiness that was "near" was a life you had put away.

GUY. The happiness that was near was a treasure

not mine to touch! I believed that treasure then
to be another's.

MRS. PEVEREL. You had too great things to think
of—and now I see how they've changed you. You
hold yourself in another way.

GUY. (*Smiling.*) I try to carry my "name"!

MRS. PEVEREL. (*Triumphant, to prove how right
she has been.*) You carry it better than you did!

GUY. People have cried me up for it. But the
better the name, the better the man should be.

MRS. PEVEREL. He can't be better than when his
duty prevails.

GUY. Sometimes that duty is darkened, and then
it shines again! It lighted my way as I came, and
it's bright in my eyes at this hour. But the bright-
ness, in truth, is *yours*—it grows and grows in your
presence. Better than anything I sought or found
is that purer passion—this calm retreat! (*Then on
an ironic movement of* MRS. PEVEREL'S.) Aye, calm,
Madam (*struck with the sight of* LORD DEVENISH'S
*white gloves*), save for *these!* I've seen them *before*
—I've touched them. (*Thinking, recalling; then
with light breaking.*) At Richmond!

MRS. PEVEREL. (*Deeply discomposed, at a loss.*)
My Lord Devenish left them.

GUY. (*Astounded.*) Was he *here?*

MRS. PEVEREL. An hour ago.

GUY. And for what?

MRS. PEVEREL. (*Seeking a pretext.*) To see Mr.
Humber.—He was passing to the West—to see a
friend—and stopped to pay me his compliments.
As Mr. Humber happened to *be* here, he had no
occasion to seek further. He asked me not to put
it about.

GUY. (*Abrupt, intense.*) What does he want of
Frank?

MRS. PEVEREL. Ah, that you must ask *him!*

GUY. (*With a start.*) His lordship? Not yet!—I must ask *Frank!*

MRS. PEVEREL. I *meant* Mr. Humber.

GUY. (*Thinking, sharply demurring. Dismissing this as impossible. Then as he sees* FANNY: *re-enter* FANNY.) Has Mr. Humber gone?

FANNY. Mr. George won't *let* him!

MRS. PEVEREL. Ask him to please come back! (*Exit* FANNY.) Can you think of no *good* motive—?

GUY. For his lordship's presence here?—Have you got one to tell me?

MRS. PEVEREL. (*Making a visibly immense, a quite pathetic effort.*) He came to let me know—

GUY. (*In suspense.*) To let you know?

MRS. PEVEREL. (*Checking herself, giving it up with a motion of disappointment.*) Mr. Humber!

(*Re-enter* FRANK HUMBER. *Exit* MRS. PEVEREL.)

GUY. (*With excited abruptness.*) I know my Lord Devenish is here!

FRANK. (*Surprised.*) Mrs. Peverel has told you?

GUY. He betrayed himself. (*Pointing to the gloves.*) For a conspirator, he's careless!

FRANK. (*Loyally feigning blankness.*) Is he a "conspirator"?

GUY. In what other character can he have stolen such an extraordinary march? (*With passionate earnestness.*) Frank—what has he come to obtain of you? It was you he came to have speech of?

FRANK. (*Grave, impenetrable.*) He has *had* it!

GUY. And to what end, please?

FRANK. To the end that I'm leaving England for ever.

GUY. (*Bewildered.*) To go where?

FRANK. Anywhere that's far enough!

GUY. (*With fresh dismay.*) For that man?

FRANK. For myself. For everyone!

GUY. (*Peremptory.*) For *me*, Frank?

FRANK. (*Still evasive.*) For peace—for life!

GUY. But at *his* strange suit—his instance?

FRANK. He thinks it right!

GUY. (*With a bitter laugh.*) What *he* thinks right won't do! He came to undermine you!

FRANK. It didn't matter—I saw my duty.

GUY. Your duty to whom?

FRANK. To myself!

GUY. If it was so clear, why were you at Porches?

FRANK. (*Passing this question by.*) And my duty to *you.* Don't I know you love her?

GUY. (*Quick.*) You didn't know till I told you!

FRANK. On the contrary, you saw I *did!*

GUY. (*Recalling, seeing clear.*) Devenish told you—betrayed me?

FRANK. He rendered you a service!

GUY. His "services" are selfish. His services are base. His offices are curst! (*Explaining to himself now completely, and as if, therefore, to* FRANK.) He got here first to practise on my freedom, on my honour. He guessed my secret, and he used it! He has driven you from home.

FRANK. Not *he,* man! My own discomfort.

GUY. Your own discomfort is his lordship's own plan—the fruit of his visit!

FRANK. The fruit of my miserable failure!

GUY. Is it your miserable failure that brings you —without a warrant—to the feet of this lady?

FRANK. I only came to tell her I'm going.

GUY. And let that danger plead for you? (*Triumphantly.*) Frank—you had a hope!

FRANK. (*After an instant, pleading guilty.*) Well, I had one spark!

GUY. Which was quick to be a flame! His lordship quenched it.

FRANK. (*Convicted, confessing.*) His lordship arrived—it went out! He told me you were free again.

GUY. "Free—free"? Free only to undo? My freedom, verily, is vast! My freedom, Frank, is wonderful! My freedom's a boon to his lordship! (*Then in a sudden different tone, still sarcastically but ominously.*) He shouldn't touch my freedom! For *me* these things are done, and for me another good man suffers?

FRANK. You did what you could for me three months ago—I'm ready to help you now.

GUY. Help me by considering that I hold you fast! I've known you long, sir: I wish you no manner of ill.

FRANK. (*Moved, perplexed.*) Then what am I to believe?

GUY. Not that I do a damage wherever I turn! I was called into the "world"—but I didn't come for sorrow! I cost no pang, as I *was!*

FRANK. My dear fellow—you don't know!

GUY. (*Struck, wondering.*) Do you know, Frank?

FRANK. (*Turning away.*) Ask me not too much! *
(*Re-enter* MRS. PEVEREL.)

MRS. PEVEREL. It's a simple case of conscience—I must free his lordship!

FRANK. He's in *there!*

GUY. (*Astonished, then smiling.*) All this while?

MRS. PEVEREL. (*Gravely.*) He has had patience!

GUY. (*Imperatively checking her.*) He'll have to have more! There's something I wish to say to you

---

* At this point James wrote the following speech for Guy, later deleting it:

GUY. (*Gazing before him; visionary.*) I only see what I see! Such a counsel—was *no* counsel; such a duty—was none! They offered me "life"! But "life"—for *me*—is evil! It's planted in a sacrifice of others. I put that away yesterday, to meet it again to-day. (*With clear resolution.*) I put it away once more—for a sacrifice that's all my own. The high call I obeyed had a hidden vice, a fatal flaw, which the *other* call has not. It was all a wild error—a wild error from the first; a dark sophistication—and a snare! I bend, Frank, to my lesson!

first. (*To* FRANK.) Will you do me the favour of
letting his lordship know that I've arrived and of
asking him if I may wait upon him? (*Exit* FRANK
*to the bookroom. After an instant, solemnly.*) I'm
the last of the Domvilles! Three months ago—in
that dear old garden—you spoke to me, with eloquence, for my line. *I* believed what you said to me
—and I went forth into the world to test it. That
belief has passed away. But the older, the higher
abides. I tried to forget it—I did my best. But in
this place again (*looking round him as if with the
rush of old memories*) it comes back to me, it
surrounds me. It looks me in the face, and it looks
with reproachful eyes.

MRS. PEVEREL. There should be no reproach
for *you,* Mr. Domville—because you're heroic.

GUY. We *talked* of heroism here—when we talked
of renouncement.

MRS. PEVEREL. But the hour came when *against*
renouncement—I lifted my feeble voice.

GUY. Your voice was sweet to me—and it's sweeter
than ever now.

MRS. PEVEREL. Yours has a tone, Mr. Domville,
that's different—that's strange.

GUY. It sounds strange to myself, believe me,
when I ask you—to let me plead again—for Frank.
Take pity on him—don't send him forth from his
home.

MRS. PEVEREL. You speak for him as if— (*Breaking
down with excess of feeling. Re-enter* FRANK HUM-
BER *and* LORD DEVENISH.)

GUY. As if I didn't love you to passion—heaven
hear me! And as if—heaven hear me!—I hadn't
come down here to *tell* you so!

FRANK. Tell her so—tell her so, Guy. And if
"heaven" *doesn't* forgive you I'll set heaven an
example.

GUY. As if I spoke without an effort and held my

peace without a pang? I grant you freely, Madam, it wasn't for *that,* I came.

FRANK. He came on a mighty different business!

GUY. I came for a good thing, but I shall have found occasion for a better, and I think that in all the future I shall have an equal joy of both! It is *I* who shall go!

LORD DEVENISH. I've consented, sir, to meet you.

GUY. I'm the *last,* my lord, of the Domvilles! (*Then anticipating* DEVENISH'S *reply and speaking on his quick gesture of impatient despair.*) You've been so good as to take a zealous interest in my future—and in that of my family: for which I owe you, and now ask you to accept, all *thanks.* But I beg you, still more solemnly, to let that prodigious zeal rest, from this moment, for ever! I listened to your accents for a day—I followed you where you led me. I looked at life as you showed it, and then I turned away my face. That's why I stand here again; for (*with intensely controlled emotion*) there are other things—there are partings. (*Then very gently to* MRS. PEVEREL.) Will my conveyance have come back?

MRS. PEVEREL. (*Listening an instant, and as if subjugated by his returning sanctity.*) I think I hear it now.

GUY. Then I start this moment for Bristol. (*Sadly, kindly smiling.*) Father Murray has had patience. I go with him to France, to take up my work in the Church! if the Church will *take* again an erring son!

MRS. PEVEREL. She'll take him.

LORD DEVENISH. And *you* give him?

MRS. PEVEREL. To *her!*

LORD DEVENISH. (*With high sarcasm, to* GUY.) I hope you do justice to this lady's exemplary sacrifice!

GUY. (*Blank.*) Sacrifice?

LORD DEVENISH. That of a sentiment my consideration for her forbids me to name.

FRANK. She loves you, Guy!

LORD DEVENISH. He doesn't deserve to know it. (*Then smiling, gallant to* MRS. PEVEREL.) If it were *me,* Madam! (*From the threshold.*) Pity me!

MRS. PEVEREL. It was a dream, but the dream is past!

GUY. (*Gathering himself slowly from a deep, stupefied commotion.*) The Church *takes* me! (*To* MRS. PEVEREL.) Be kind to him. (*To* FRANK.) Be good to her. (*At the door.*) Be good to her.

FRANK. Mrs. Peverel—I shall *hope!*

MRS. PEVEREL. Wait!

# III

## The Critics

BERNARD SHAW
H. G. WELLS
ARNOLD BENNETT

# BERNARD SHAW

## THE DRAMA'S LAWS

*Saturday Review,* January 12, 1895

THE TRUTH about Mr. James's play is no worse than that it is out of fashion. Any dramatically disposed young gentleman who, cultivating sentiment on a little alcohol, and gaining an insight to the mysteries of the eternal feminine by a couple of squalid intrigues, meanwhile keeps well aloof from art and philosophy, and thus preserves his innocence of the higher life of the senses and of the intellect, can patch up a play to-morrow which will pass as real drama with the gentlemen who deny that distinction to the work of Mr. Henry James. No doubt, if the literary world were as completely dominated by the admirers of Mr. Rider Haggard as the dramatic world is by their first cousins, we should be told that Mr. James cannot write a novel. That is not criticism; it is a mere begging of the question. There is no reason why life as we find it in Mr. James's novels—life, that is, in which passion is subordinate to intellect and to fastidious artistic taste—should not be represented on the stage. If it is real to Mr. James, it must be real to others; and why should not these others have their drama instead of being banished from the theatre (to the theatre's great loss) by the monotony and vulgarity of drama in which passion is everything, intellect nothing, and art only brought in by the incidental outrages upon it? As it happens, I am not myself in Mr. James's camp: in all the life that has energy enough to be interesting to me, subjective volition, passion, will, make intellect the merest tool. But there is in the centre of that cyclone a certain calm spot where cultivated ladies and gentlemen live on independent incomes or by pleasant artistic occupations. It is there that Mr. James's art touches life, selecting whatever is graceful, exquisite, or dignified in its serenity. It is not life as imagined by the pit or gallery, or even by the stalls: it is, let us say, the ideal of the balcony; but that is no reason why the pit and gallery should excommunicate it on the ground that it has no blood and entrails in it, and have its sentence formulated for it by the fiercely ambitious and wilful professional man in the stalls. The whole case against its adequacy really rests on its violation of the cardinal stage convention that love is the most irresistible of all the passions. Since most people go to the theatre to escape from reality, this convention is naturally dear to a world in which love, all powerful in the secret, unreal, day-dreaming life of the imagination, is in the real active life the abject slave of every trifling habit, prejudice, and cowardice, easily stifled by shyness, class feeling, and pecuniary prudence, or diverted from what is theatrically assumed to be its hurricane course by such obstacles as a thick ankle, a cockney accent, or an unfashionable hat. In the face of this, is it good sense to accuse Mr. Henry James of a want of grip of the realities of life because he gives us a hero who sacrifices his love to a strong and noble vocation for the Church? And yet when some unmannerly playgoer, untouched by either love or religion, chooses to send a derisive howl from the gallery at such a situation, we are to sorrowfully admit, if you please, that Mr. James is no dramatist, on the general ground that "the drama's laws the drama's patrons give." Pray which of its patrons? —the cultivated majority who, like myself and all the ablest of my colleagues, applauded Mr. James on Saturday, or the handful of rowdies who brawled at him? It is the business of the dramatic critic to educate these dunces, not to echo them.

Admitting, then, that Mr. James's dramatic authorship is valid, and that his plays are *du théâtre* when the right people are in the theatre, what are the qualities and faults of "Guy Domville"? First among the qualities, a rare charm of speech. Line after line comes with such a delicate turn and fall that I unhesitatingly challenge any of our popular dramatists to write a scene in verse with half the beauty of Mr. James's prose. I am not now speaking of the verbal fitness, which is a matter of careful workmanship merely. I am speaking of the delicate inflexions of feeling conveyed by the cadences of the line, inflexions and cadences which, after so long a course of the ordinary theatrical splashes and daubs of passion and emphasis, are as grateful to my ear as the music of Mozart's "Entführung aus dem Serail" would be after a year of "Ernani" and "Il Trovatore." Second, "Guy Domville" is a story, and not a mere situation hung out on a gallows of plot. And it is a story of fine sentiment and delicate manners, with an entirely worthy and touching ending. Third, it relies on the performers, not for the brute force of their personalities and popularities, but for their finest accomplishments in grace of manner, delicacy of diction, and dignity of style. It is pleasant to be able to add that this reliance, rash as it undeniably is in these days, was not disappointed. Mr. Alexander, having been treated little better than a tailor's dummy by Mr. Wilde, Mr. Pinero, and Mr. Henry Arthur Jones successively, found himself treated as an artist by Mr. James, and repaid the compliment, not only, as his manager, by a charming eighteenth-century stage setting of the piece, but, as actor, by his fine execution of the principal part, which he touched with great skill and judgment. Miss Marion Terry, as Mrs. Peverel, was altogether charming; every movement, every tone, harmonized perfectly with the dainty grace and feeling of her lines. In fact, had the second act been equal to the first and third, and the acting as fine throughout as in the scenes between Mr. Alexander and Miss Terry (in which, by the way, they were well supported by Mr. Waring), the result would have been less doubtful. It will be a deplorable misfortune if "Guy Domville" does not hold the stage long enough to justify Mr. Alexander's enterprise in producing it.

Unfortunately, the second act dissolved the charm rather badly; and what was more, the actors felt it. The Falstaffian make-up of Mrs. Saker, and the senseless drunken scene, which Mr. Alexander played with the sobriety of desperation, made fuss instead of drama; and the dialogue, except for a brief and very pretty episode in which Miss Millard and Mr. Esmond took part, fell off into mere rococo. Little of this act can be remembered with pleasure except Miss Millard's "Forgive me a little," and a few cognate scraps of dialogue. It had better have been left out, and the wanderings of the prodigal taken for granted. And, to weight it still further, it contained a great deal of the gentleman who played Lord Devenish, and played him just as he might have played an elderly marquis in a comic opera, grimacing over a snuff-box, and withering all sense and music out of Mr. James's lines with a diction which I forbear to describe. He was very largely responsible for the irritation which subsequently vented itself on the author; and I am

far from sure that I ought not to borrow a weapon
from the Speaker of the House of Commons, and
go to the extreme length of naming him.

"Guy Domville" is preceded by a farce (called in
the bill a comedy) by Julian Field, entitled "Too
Happy by Half." It is deftly turned out from old
and seasoned materials, and is capital fun for the
audience and for Mr. Esmond and Miss Millard.
Miss Millard is not yet quite experienced enough
to do very easy work quite well: she is the least
bit crude occasionally.

# H. G. WELLS

## A PRETTY QUESTION

*Pall Mall Gazette,* January 7, 1895

MR. HENRY JAMES has selected for his theme an
excursion into the world, a "voyage of discovery"
for three brief months, taken by a young man
trained as a priest, and for his period the picturesque days immediately preceding the French
Revolution. Guy Domville, private tutor to the son
of the young and beautiful widow, Mrs. Peverel,
is preparing to leave that position to enter the
Roman Catholic Church, when an unexpected
hunting accident terminates the elder branch of
the family and makes him the "last of the Domvilles." The first intimation of this is brought to
him at Mrs. Peverel's house by that elderly and
impoverished nobleman, Lord Devenish. This Lord
Devenish is the Mephistopheles of the excursion;
he appeals to Guy's family pride, to his youthful
love of life, and skilfully induces Mrs. Peverel to
help in dissuading Guy from the cloister. Mrs.
Peverel loves Guy and Guy loves Mrs. Peverel, but
having been requested in the Miles Standish fashion
to undertake the case of Frank Humber, he apparently considers himself in honour bound to forego
her. He accompanies Lord Devenish to London, sees
life, and appears in the second act sadly changed,
no longer an earthly saint, but a very brilliant and

accomplished gentleman in scarlet and steel. He gambles and drinks freely, and is about to be married, quite against her will, to Mary Brasier, the reputed daughter of a cousin by marriage. Really, however, Mary is the child of an intrigue between Lord Devenish and Mrs. Domville, her mother. George Round (Lieutenant R.N.), the courier and accepted lover of Mary, returns on the morning of the marriage. He moors his boat at the back of Mrs. Domville's house—it is at Richmond —early in the second act, and comes and goes with great freedom and pertinacity through the conservatory. Then follows a remarkable scene: Round pretends to be drunk and tries to make Guy Domville really so; Domville perceives his intention, pours away the wine into a bowl of flowers, and also pretends to be drunk. His pretence successfully deceives Round, but not Mary. However, after numerous exits and entrances it ends happily in Domville understanding how matters lie, and Round retires to his boat for the last time through Domville's apartments, with Mary, presumably to fly to Twickenham and marry. Therewith Domville leaves London in a fit of disgust, and returns to the pining Mrs. Peverel. This second act is the weak part of the play. It is tedious and impossible; people come and go in the house unchallenged, like rabbits in a warren, and it was played with a singular lack of spirit. Moreover, as it was acted there was scarcely a hint of Guy's growing disgust with life, especially of such life as Lord Devenish typifies, a disgust that forms the key to the third act.

Lord Devenish, after the collapse of his marriage scheme, for no earthly reason, hurries off to Mrs. Peverel to tell her of the business. Guy arrives while he is there, and the nobleman, being anxious to escape him, is hustled off into another room. Guy is proposing marriage to Mrs. Peverel, when he discovers the glove of Lord Devenish on the table. It is the taint of the world, and in a passionate revulsion he resolves to proceed to his monastery, commending Frank Humber to Mrs. Peverel in his last farewell.

It is [a] fine conception, but altogether too weakly developed. The circumstances of Guy's disillusionment are quite inadequate, and that and the complexity of the second act are the faults of Mr. James. But the play fails chiefly through the imperfect appreciation of the players. A less convincing performance than that of Mr. Elliot as the subtle and scheming Lord Devenish it would be hard to imagine. He is made up in a mode of caricature, and presents the extreme of fashionable folly —he might have come out of Hogarth, but he has certainly no business to come into this play. In the first act Mr. Alexander, as Guy Domville, is a didactic puritan; in the second a fine generous blade; in the third he is that impossible, noble, iron-grey Mr. Alexander that we have seen before. Then it was Mrs. Saker's business to be a woman of fifty—a duty she has neglected; and she wears a costume that may possibly be historically correct, but which was incredible to half the audience, and which touches the note of caricature at absolutely the wrong moment. To the rest of the cast, however, no objection can be raised. They did their work decently and in order.

The play was received with marked disapproval by a considerable section of the audience. Yet it was, save for the defects we have pointed out, a play finely conceived and beautifully written. But the entire workmanship was too delicate for acting; and whether that is the fault of player or playwright is a very pretty question. A play written for the stage may very well be compared to a pen-and-ink drawing that is to undergo reproduction by some cheap photographic process. Delicate turns, soft shades, refinements of grey *must* be avoided; bold strokes, black and firm—that is all that is possible. The thing is to be reproduced on such a scale as to carry across unimpaired to the pit and gallery. Delicate work simply blurs and looks weak. The better the process, of course, the finer the work it will render; with such acting as one may dream of, this play might still have been a very beautiful one in spite of its structural defect. But as it was, it is undeniable that the delicacy of the play degenerated into a hectic weakness; and of all defects feebleness is the one most abhorred of the gods. The diagnosis points to an early deathbed; only a tonic treatment and the utmost gentleness on the part of those concerned in it can save the life of the play. Mr. Elliot in particular must moderate his grimaces, and Mrs. Saker must be toned down. And for the tonic treatment—that is for Mr. James and Mr. Alexander to consider. As it stands at present, the second act is hopeless, and the mental evolution of Guy Domville altogether incredible.

# ARNOLD BENNETT

## FITFUL BEAUTY

*Woman,* January 16, 1895

THE BEHAVIOUR of the pit and gallery at the
production by Mr. George Alexander, at the St.
James's Theatre, of Mr. Henry James's play *Guy
Domville* was to me quite inexplicable. The piece
is assuredly not faultless—far from it; but it is so
beautifully written, it contains so many exquisite
scenes, it is so conscientiously and artistically acted,
and so lavishly staged, that the *longueurs* of the
second act, one would have thought, might have
been either forgiven or endured in respectful silence. I avoided coming to any hasty conclusions,
and therefore deferred my notice until this week.
The period of the play is 1780. In the first act we
find ourselves in the garden of Porches, where dwell
Mrs. Peverel (Miss Marion Terry), a beautiful
widow, her little son, and the boy's tutor, Guy
Domville (Mr. George Alexander). Guy, though
the bearer of an ancient name, is poor; we see him
upon the point of taking Holy Orders. Everything
is, in fact, arranged, when enter Lord Devenish, a
messenger from Mrs. Domville, Guy's cousin's wife,
to say that through a hunting accident Guy is the
last male of his line, and heir to rich, though encumbered, possessions. Lord Devenish (Mr. Elliot)
urges Guy that it is his duty now to give up the

Church and marry, in order to carry on the great
family traditions. The conflict between Church and
family is movingly displayed. The family wins, and
Guy sets off for London with Lord Devenish, whose
interest in him, by the way, may be attributed to
the fact that the aristocratic and rascally old *viveur*
is in love with Mrs. Domville, and has obtained
her promise to marry him if he can bring about a
marriage between Guy and Mary Brasier, Mrs.
Domville's daughter by her first husband.

Guy goes to London, half aware that he is in
love with Mrs. Peverel, who is undoubtedly in love
with him, though she has almost promised herself
to Frank Humber (Mr. Herbert Waring), an excellent young squire in the neighbourhood, whose suit
Guy has himself pleaded. The second act is tedious.
We meet Guy gaily dressed, in the full enjoyment
of life and betrothed to Mary Brasier (Miss Evelyn
Millard). But Mary is in love with a young naval
lieutenant, George Round (Mr. H. V. Esmond),
and when, through plot and counterplot, and after
much mock drunkenness between himself and
Round, Guy gets to know of this, he assists the pair
to make an entirely preposterous and impossible
elopement, and sets off to return to Porches with a
heart full of hatred for Lord Devenish and his
scheming paramour, Mrs. Domville. Lord Devenish
suddenly discovers that it will suit his and Mrs.
Domville's plans just as well if Guy marries Mrs.
Peverel. So he posts to Porches, gets there first, and
advises Mrs. Peverel to marry Guy. While they are
conversing Guy is announced, and Lord Devenish
hides in the library. There is a beautiful scene between Mrs. Peverel and the returned wanderer, and
Guy is just making open love to her when he sees
Lord Devenish's glove on the table. So Devenish has
his finger in this pie also! If Devenish wants him
to marry Mrs. Peverel then he will not marry her.

The claims of his deserted Church rush in upon him, and he goes away to seek ordination, his last words being a request to Mrs. Peverel to accept Frank Humber.

Such, brief and imperfectly, is the plot. The defects of its motivation will be only too apparent. The whole business of Lord Devenish and his schemes is quite "too thin." Why should a man of his habits, admittedly a guilty lover, and, indeed, the father of Mary, wish to marry Mrs. Domville at all? And, his plan for the bartering of his daughter having failed, how comes it about that it will suit him equally well if Guy marries Mrs. Peverel? The answer is clearly: These things are so in order that the play may not come to a dead stop. In the first act, the absurdity of Lord Devenish's interference in the Domvilles' affairs is not completely apparent, and consequently it is the best act of the three: natural, impressive, and studded with gems of dialogue—gems, however, of too modest and serene a beauty to suit the taste of an audience accustomed to the scintillating gauds of Mr. Oscar Wilde and Mr. H. A. Jones. The second act is invertebrate, long-winded, and impossible; and it clearly shows that either of the aforenamed gentlemen, though they may be vastly inferior to Mr. James as literary artists, could yet give him some valuable lessons upon plot-weaving. When one considers the unrivalled work which Mr. James has produced in fiction, one marvels that he should have allowed this second act to get outside his study. For the elopement of Mary and the lieutenant, arranged in a moment, and, we are to suppose, carried out with complete success, is really childish; there is neither rhyme nor reason in it. The third act is fitfully beautiful, and the closing scene, did we not suspect that it was quite unnecessary, most touching.

As for the acting, Mr. Alexander carried off the honours. His performance was probably the best thing he has done; it need only be pointed out that his budding priest was more artistic than his man of the world. Miss Marion Terry, with the Terry voice and movement, could not fail to be charming as the widow, and she showed a fine intellectual grasp of the part. Mr. Herbert Waring, not a villain this time, was admirable as Frank Humber. Miss Millard had small scope, appearing only in one act, as the eloping maiden, but what she did she did meetly. Miss Irene Vanbrugh worked marvels with the little part of Mrs. Peverel's maid; while Mrs. Edward Saker, as the despicable Mrs. Domville, was far, far from successful. Mr. Elliot as Lord Devenish, and Mr. Esmond as the lieutenant, were neither good nor bad. A final word of appreciation for the scenery. The setting of the last act, the "white parlour" at Mrs. Peverel's home, Porches, was one of the most perfect stage interiors I have ever seen.

# A NOTE ON THE TEXT
## OF *GUY DOMVILLE*

THE TYPESCRIPT is at Harvard in the Houghton Library.

The printed prompt-book follows closely the typescript with only a few minor alterations such as, "Leave him with me," changed to read, "Leave me with him," and substitution of a few phrases and words for greater clarity. The following copies of the prompt-book were examined:

(a) A copy in the Lord Chamberlain's office, London, containing no alterations and marked as licensed for production on December 10, 1894.

(b) A copy in the Houghton Library. This was Henry James's and contains a number of corrections in his hand. At the Houghton there is to be found a sheaf of manuscript in James's hand, individual sheets containing a series of corrections and alterations made by the novelist. These were copied into the prompt-books, apparently by a copyist or secretary at the theatre, and this explains the fact that other copies which have turned up in the rare book market are interleaved and contain numerous textual changes.

(c) A copy in the Henry E. Huntington Library, San Marino, California, interleaved and containing the corrections and alterations of the loose sheets described in (b) written in by three hands, one of them James's. The majority of changes, however, are not in James's hand but in a handwriting resembling that of other similar copies. James's autograph changes are on pp. 18, 19, 26, 31, 53, 55, 78, 79.

(d) Marion Terry's copy, interleaved and corrected in a similar fashion to (c), now at the Colby College Library, Waterville, Maine.

The text of *Guy Domville* published in this volume includes all the alterations in Henry James's copy as well as those contained in the miscellaneous manuscript sheets at Harvard and in addition such alterations as are in the Huntington Library copy which do not occur elsewhere.

# DATE DUE

|  |  |
|---|---|
|  |  |
|  |  |
|  |  |
|  |  |
|  |  |
|  |  |
|  |  |
|  |  |
|  |  |
|  |  |
|  |  |
|  |  |
|  |  |
|  |  |
|  |  |
|  |  |
|  |  |
|  |  |
|  |  |
|  |  |
|  |  |